YOUR PERSONAL
HOROSCOPE
2007

SAGITTARIUS

Your Personal Horoscope 2007

Sagittarius

23rd November–21st December

igloo

igloo

This edition published by Igloo Books Ltd,
Garrard Way, Kettering, NN16 8TD
www.igloo-books.com
E-mail: Info@igloo-books.com

Produced for Igloo Books by W. Foulsham & Co. Ltd,
The Publishing House, Bennetts Close, Cippenham,
Slough, Berkshire SL1 5AP, England

ISBN 13: 978-1-84561-345-7
ISBN 10: 1-84561-345-7

Copyright © 2006 W. Foulsham & Co. Ltd

Printed in China

CONTENTS

1   Introduction   7

2   The Essence of Sagittarius:
    Exploring the Personality of Sagittarius the Archer   9

3   Sagittarius on the Cusp   15

4   Sagittarius and its Ascendants   17

5   The Moon and the Part it Plays in your Life   31

6   Moon Signs   35

7   Sagittarius in Love   39

8   Venus: The Planet of Love   43

9   Venus through the Zodiac Signs   45

10 Sagittarius: 2006 Diary Pages   49

11 Sagittarius: 2007 Diary Pages   71

12 Sagittarius: 2007 In Brief   72

13 Rising Signs for Sagittarius   157

14 The Zodiac, Planets and Correspondences   159

INTRODUCTION

Your Personal Horoscopes have been specifically created to allow you to get the most from astrological patterns and the way they have a bearing on not only your zodiac sign, but nuances within it. Using the diary section of the book you can read about the influences and possibilities of each and every day of the year. It will be possible for you to see when you are likely to be cheerful and happy or those times when your nature is in retreat and you will be more circumspect. The diary will help to give you a feel for the specific 'cycles' of astrology and the way they can subtly change your day-to-day life. For example, when you see the sign ☿, this means that the planet Mercury is retrograde at that time. Retrograde means it appears to be running backwards through the zodiac. Such a happening has a significant effect on communication skills, but this is only one small aspect of how the Personal Horoscope can help you.

With Your Personal Horoscope the story doesn't end with the diary pages. It includes simple ways for you to work out the zodiac sign the Moon occupied at the time of your birth, and what this means for your personality. In addition, if you know the time of day you were born, it is possible to discover your Ascendant, yet another important guide to your personal make-up and potential.

Many readers are interested in relationships and in knowing how well they get on with people of other astrological signs. You might also be interested in the way you appear to very different sorts of individuals. If you are such a person, the section on Venus will be of particular interest. Despite the rapidly changing position of this planet, you can work out your Venus sign, and learn what bearing it will have on your life.

Using Your Personal Horoscope you can travel on one of the most fascinating and rewarding journeys that anyone can take – the journey to a better realisation of self.

THE ESSENCE
OF SAGITTARIUS

Exploring the Personality of Sagittarius the Archer

(23RD NOVEMBER – 21ST DECEMBER)

What's in a sign?

Sagittarius is ruled by the large, expansive planet Jupiter, which from an astrological perspective makes all the difference to this happy-go-lucky and very enterprising zodiac sign. This is the sign of the Archer and there is a very good reason for our ancient ancestors having chosen the half-man, half-horse figure with its drawn bow. Not only are Sagittarians fleet-footed like a horse, but the remarks they make, like the arrow, go right to the target.

You love contentious situations and rarely shy away from controversy. With tremendous faith in your own abilities you are not easily kept down, and would usually find it relatively simple to persuade others to follow your course. Though you are born of a Fire sign, you are not as bullying as Aries can be, or as proud as a Leo. Despite this you do have a Fire-sign temper and can be a formidable opponent once you have your dander up.

You rarely choose to take the long route to any destination in life, preferring to drive forward as soon as your mind is made up. Communication comes easy to you and you add to your stock of weapons good intuitive insight and a capacity for brinkmanship that appears to know no bounds. At your best you are earnest, aspiring and honourable, though on the other side of the coin Sagittarians can make the best con artists of all!

What you hate most is to be discouraged, or for others to thwart your intentions. There is a slight tendency for you to use others whilst you are engaging in many of the schemes that are an intrinsic part of your life, though you would never deliberately hurt or offend anyone.

Sagittarian people are natural lovers of fun. When what is required is a shot of enthusiasm, or an immediacy that can cut right through the middle of any red tape, it is the Archer who invariably ends up in charge. When others panic, you come into your own, and you have an ability to get things done in a quarter of the expected time. Whether they are completed perfectly, however, is a different matter altogether.

Sagittarius resources

Sagittarians appear to be the natural conjurors of the zodiac. The stage magician seems to draw objects from thin air, and it often appears that the Archer is able to do something similar. This is an intriguing process to observe, but somewhat difficult to explain. Sagittarians seem to be able to get directly to the heart of any matter, and find it easy to circumnavigate potential difficulties. Thus they achieve objectives that look impossible to observers – hence the conjuring analogy.

Just as the biblical David managed to defeat Goliath with nothing more than a humble pebble and a sling, Sagittarius also goes seemingly naked into battle. The Archer relies on his or her natural wit, together with a fairly instinctive intelligence, a good deal of common sense and a silver tongue. The patient observer must inevitably come to the conclusion that what really matters isn't what the Sagittarian can do, but how much they manage to get others to undertake on their behalf. In other words, people follow your lead without question. This quality can be one of your best resources and only fails when you have doubt about yourself, which fortunately is very rarely.

If other signs could sell refrigerators to Eskimos, you could add a deep-freeze complete with ice tray! This is one of the reasons why so many Archers are engaged in both advertising and marketing. Not only do you know what people want, you also have an instinctive ability to make them want whatever it is you have on offer.

It is likely that you would see nothing remotely mysterious about your ability to peer through to the heart of any matter. In the main you would refer to this as 'gut reaction', despite the fact that it looks distinctly magical to those around you. Fortunately this is part of your mystique, and even if you should choose to take someone for a complete ride, it is doubtful that they would end up disliking you as a result. You don't set out to be considered a genius, and you manage to retain the common touch. This is extremely important, for those with whom you have contacts actively want to help you because you are a 'regular guy'.

Beneath the surface

People tend to be very complicated. Untangling their motives in any given situation is rarely easy. Psychologists have many theories regarding the working of the human psyche and philosophers have struggled with such matters for thousands of years. Clearly none of these people were looking at the zodiac sign of Sagittarius. Ask the average Archer why they did this or that thing and the chances are that you will get a reply something very similar to 'Well, it seemed like a good idea at the time'.

While many people might claim to be uncomplicated, at heart you genuinely are. Complications are something you try to avoid, even though some of your deals in life might look like a roll of barbed wire to those around you. In the main you keep your objectives as simple as possible. This is one of the reasons why it isn't particularly difficult for you to circumnavigate some of the potential pitfalls – you simply won't recognise that they exist. Setting your eyes on the horizon you set off with a jaunty step, refusing to acknowledge problems and, when necessary, sorting them out on the way.

Your general intention is to succeed and this fact permeates just about every facet of your life. Satisfaction doesn't necessarily come for you from a job well done, because the word 'well' in this context often isn't especially important. And when you have one task out of the way, you immediately set your sights on something else. Trying to figure out exactly why you live your life in the way you do, your psychological imperatives and ultimate intentions, costs you too much time, so you probably don't indulge in such idle speculation at all.

You have a warm heart and always want the best for everyone. It almost never occurs to you that other people don't think about things in the way you might and you automatically assume that others will be only too pleased to follow your lead. In the main you are uncomplicated, don't indulge in too many frills and fancies and speak your mind. There really isn't much difference between what you do in life, and what you think about your actions. This is not to infer that you are shallow, merely that you don't see much point in complicating the obvious with too much internal musing.

One of the main reasons why people like you so much is because the 'what you see is what you get' adage is more true in your case than in any other.

11

Making the best of yourself

Always on the go and invariably looking for a new challenge, it isn't hard to see how Sagittarius makes the best of itself. This is a dynamic, thrusting sign, with a thirst for adventure and a great ability to think on its feet. As a child of Sagittarius you need the cut and thrust of an exciting life in order to show your true mettle. It doesn't do for you to sit around inactive for any length of time and any sort of enforced lay-off is likely to drive you to distraction.

In a career situation your natural proclivities show through, so it's best for you to be in some position which necessitates decision making on a moment-by-moment basis. Production-line work or tasks that involve going over the same ground time and again are not really your forte, though you are certainly not afraid of hard work and can labour on regardless towards any objective – just as long as there is a degree of excitement on the way.

Socially speaking you probably have many friends, and that's the way you like things to be. You need to know that people rate you highly, and will usually be on hand to offer the sort of advice that is always interesting, but probably not totally reasoned. It's a fact that you think everyone has the same ability to think on their feet that typifies your nature, and you trust everyone instinctively – at least once.

In love you need the sort of relationship that allows a degree of personal freedom. You can't be fettered and so have to be your own person under all situations. You are kind and attentive, though sometimes get carried away with the next grand scheme and so you need an understanding partner. Archers should not tie themselves down too early in life and are at their best surrounded by those who love the dynamism and difficult-to-predict qualities exemplified by this zodiac sign.

Most important of all you need to be happy with your lot. Living through restricted or miserable times takes its toll. Fortunately these are few in your life, mainly because of the effort you put into life yourself.

The impressions you give

You must be doing something right because it's a fact that Sagittarius represents one of the most instinctively liked zodiac signs. There are many reasons for this state of affairs. For starters you will always do others a good turn if it's possible. It's true that you are a bit of a rogue on occasions, but that only endears you to the sort of individuals with whom you choose to share your life. You are always the first with a joke, even under difficult circumstances, and you face problems with an open mind and a determination to get through them. On the way you acquire many friends, though in your case many 'acquaintances' might be nearer the mark. This is a situation of your own choosing and though you have so much to recommend you to others, it's a fact that you keep really close ties to the absolute minimum.

Some people might think you rather superficial and perhaps an intellectual lightweight. If so, this only comes about because they don't understand the way your mind works. All the same it is your own nature that leads a few individuals to these conclusions. You can skip from one subject to another, are an insatiable flirt in social situations and love to tell funny stories. 'Depth' isn't really your thing and that means that you could appear to lower the tone of conversations that are getting too heavy for your liking. You do need to be the centre of attention most of the time, which won't exactly endear you to others who have a similar disposition.

People know that you have a temper, like all Fire signs. They will also realise that your outbursts are rare, short-lived and of no real note. You don't bear a grudge and quickly learn that friends are more useful than enemies under any circumstance.

You come across as the capricious, bubbly, lively, likeable child of the zodiac and under such circumstances it would be very difficult for anyone to find fault with you for long. Often outrageous, always interesting and seldom down in the dumps – it's hard to see how you could fail to be loved.

The way forward

It might be best to realise, right from the outset, that you are not indestructible. Deep inside you have all the same insecurities, vulnerabilities and paranoia that the rest of humanity possesses. As a Sagittarian it doesn't do to dwell on such matters, but at least the acknowledgement might stop you going over the edge sometimes. You come from a part of the zodiac that has to be active and which must show itself in the best possible light all the time, and that's a process that is very demanding.

In the main, however, you relish the cut and thrust of life and it is quite likely that you already have the necessary recipe for happiness and success. If you don't, then you are involved in a search that is likely to be both interesting and rewarding, because it isn't really the objective that matters to you but rather the fun you can have on the way.

Be as honest as you can with those around you, though without losing that slightly roguish charm that makes you so appealing. At the same time try to ensure that your own objectives bear others in mind. You can sometimes be a little fickle and, in rare circumstances, unscrupulous. At heart though, you have your own moral convictions and would rarely do anyone a bad turn. On the contrary, you do your best to help those around you, and invariably gain in popularity on the way.

Health-wise you are probably fairly robust but you can run your nervous system into the ground on occasions. There are times when a definite routine suits you physically, but this doesn't always agree with your mental make-up, which is essentially driving and demanding. The peaks and troughs of your life are an inevitable part of what makes you tick, and you would be a poorer person without them.

Explaining yourself is not generally difficult, and neither is the search for personal success, even if you keep looking beyond it to even greater achievements further down the road. Being loved is important, despite the fact that you would deny this on occasions. Perhaps you don't always know yourself as well as you might, though since you are not an inveterate deep thinker it is likely that this is not a problem to you.

If you are already an adult, it's likely the path you are presently following is the one for you. That doesn't mean to say that you will keep to it, or find it universally rewarding. You find new promise in each day, and that's the joy of Sagittarius.

SAGITTARIUS ON THE CUSP

Astrological profiles are altered for those people born at either the beginning or the end of a zodiac sign, or, more properly, on the cusps of a sign. In the case of Sagittarius this would be on the 23rd of November and for two or three days after, and similarly at the end of the sign, probably from the 19th to the 21st of December.

The Scorpio Cusp – November 23rd to 25th

You could turn out to be one of the most well-liked people around, especially if you draw heavily from the more positive qualities of the two zodiac signs that have the most profound part to play in your life. Taken alone the Sagittarian is often accused of being rather too flighty. Sagittarians are often guilty of flirting and sometimes fall foul of people who take a more serious view of life in general. The presence in your make-up of the much deeper and more contemplative sign of Scorpio brings a quiet and a sense of reserve that the Sagittarian nature sometimes lacks. Although you like to have a good time and would be more than willing to dance the night away, you are probably also happy enough when the time comes to go home. Family means much to you and you have a great sensitivity to the needs of those around you. What makes all the difference is that you not only understand others, but you have the potential to take practical steps to help them.

You are probably not quite the workaholic that the Archer alone tends to be and can gain rest and relaxation, which has to be good for you in the longer term. You don't lack the ability to be successful but your level of application is considered, less frenetic and altogether more ordered. It's true that some confusion comes into your life from time to time, but you have the resources to deal with such eventualities, and you do so with a smile on your face most of the time. People would warm to you almost instantly and you are likely to do whatever you can to support family members and friends.

Often sinking into a dream world if you feel threatened, some of the achievements that are second nature to the Sagittarian are left on the shelf for a while. There are times when this turns out to be a blessing, if only because your actions are more considered. Personality clashes with others are less likely with this combination and Sagittarius also modifies the slightly moody qualities that come with Scorpio alone. More methodical in every way than the usual Archer, in many situations you are a good combination of optimist and pessimist.

15

The Capricorn Cusp – December 19th to 21st

The fact that comes across almost immediately with the Capricorn cusp of Sagittarius is how very practical you tend to be. Most of you would be ideal company on a desert island, for a number of reasons. Firstly you are quite self-contained, which Sagittarius taken alone certainly is not. You would soon get your head round the practical difficulties of finding food and shelter, and would be very happy to provide these necessities for your companions too. Unlike the typical Sagittarian you do not boast and probably do not come across as being quite so overbearing as the Archer seems to be. For all this you are friendly, chatty, love to meet many different and interesting types and do whatever you can to be of assistance to a world which is all the better for having you in it.

There is less of a tendency for you to worry at a superficial level than Sagittarius alone is inclined to do, mainly because long periods of practical application bring with them a contemplative tendency that Sagittarius sometimes lacks. In love you tend to be quite sincere, even if the slightly fickle tendencies of the Archer do show through now and again. Any jealousy that is levelled at you by your partner could be as a result of your natural attractiveness, which you probably don't seek. Fairly comfortable in almost any sort of company, you are at your best when faced with individuals who have something intelligent and interesting to say. As a salesperson you would be second to none, but it would be essential for you to believe absolutely in the product or service you were selling.

Almost any sort of work is possible in your case, though you wouldn't take too kindly to being restricted in any way, and need the chance to show what your practical nature is worth, as well as your keen perception and organisational abilities. What matters most for you at work is that you are well liked by others and that you manage to maintain a position of control through inspiring confidence. On a creative level, the combination of Sagittarius and Capricorn would make you a good sculptor, or possibly a natural landscape gardener.

SAGITTARIUS AND ITS ASCENDANTS

The nature of every individual on the planet is composed of the rich variety of zodiac signs and planetary positions that were present at the time of their birth. Your Sun sign, which in your case is Sagittarius, is one of the many factors when it comes to assessing the unique person you are. Probably the most important consideration, other than your Sun sign, is to establish the zodiac sign that was rising over the eastern horizon at the time that you were born. This is your Ascending or Rising sign. Most popular astrology fails to take account of the Ascendant, and yet its importance remains with you from the very moment of your birth, through every day of your life. The Ascendant is evident in the way you approach the world, and so, when meeting a person for the first time, it is this astrological influence that you are most likely to notice first. Our Ascending sign essentially represents what we appear to be, while the Sun sign is what we feel inside ourselves.

The Ascendant also has the potential for modifying our overall nature. For example, if you were born at a time of day when Sagittarius was passing over the eastern horizon (this would be around the time of dawn) then you would be classed as a double Sagittarius. As such, you would typify this zodiac sign, both internally and in your dealings with others. However, if your Ascendant sign turned out to be an Earth sign, such as Taurus, there would be a profound alteration of nature, away from the expected qualities of Sagittarius.

One of the reasons why popular astrology often ignores the Ascendant is that it has always been rather difficult to establish. We have found a way to make this possible by devising an easy-to-use table, which you will find on page 157 of this book. Using this, you can establish your Ascendant sign at a glance. You will need to know your rough time of birth, then it is simply a case of following the instructions.

For those readers who have no idea of their time of birth it might be worth allowing a good friend, or perhaps your partner, to read through the section that follows this introduction. Someone who deals with you on a regular basis may easily discover your Ascending sign, even though you could have some difficulty establishing it for yourself. A good understanding of this component of your nature is essential if you want to be aware of that 'other person' who is responsible for the way you make contact with the world at large. Your Sun sign, Ascendant sign, and the other pointers in this book will, together, allow you a far better understanding of what makes you tick as an individual. Peeling back the different layers of your astrological make-up can be an enlightening experience, and the Ascendant may represent one of the most important layers of all.

Sagittarius with Sagittarius Ascendant

You are very easy to spot, even in a crowd. There is hardly a more dynamic individual to be found anywhere in the length and breadth of the zodiac. You know what you want from life and have a pretty good idea about how you will get it. The fact that you are always so cocksure is a source of great wonder to those around you, but they can't see deep inside, where you are not half as certain as you appear to be. In the main you show yourself to be kind, attentive, caring and a loyal friend. To balance this, you are determined and won't be thwarted by anything.

You keep up a searing pace through life and sometimes find it difficult to understand those people who have slightly less energy. In your better moments you understand that you are unique and will wait for others to catch up. Quite often you need periods of rest in order to recharge batteries that run down through over-use, but it doesn't take you too long to get yourself back on top form. In matters of the heart you can be slightly capricious, but you are a confident lover who knows the right words and gestures. If you are ever accused of taking others for granted you might need to indulge in some self-analysis.

Sagittarius with Capricorn Ascendant

The typical Sagittarian nature is modified for the better when Capricorn is part of the deal. It's true that you manage to push forward progressively under most circumstances, but you also possess staying power and can work long and hard to achieve your objectives, most of which are carefully planned in advance. Few people have the true measure of your nature, for it runs rather deeper than appears to be the case on the surface. Routines don't bother you as much as would be the case for Sagittarius when taken alone, and you don't care if any objective takes weeks, months or even years to achieve. You are very fond of those you take to, and prove to be a capable friend, even when things get tough.

In love relationships you are steadfast and reliable, and yet you never lose the ability to entertain. Yours is a dry sense of humour which shows itself to a multitude of different people and which doesn't evaporate, even on those occasions when life gets tough. It might take you a long time to find the love of your life, but when you do there is a greater possibility of retaining the relationship for a long period. You don't tend to inherit money, but you can easily make it for yourself, though you don't worry too much about the amount. On the whole you are self-sufficient and sensible.

Sagittarius with Aquarius Ascendant

There is an original streak to your nature which is very attractive to the people with whom you share your life. Always different, ever on the go and anxious to try out the next experiment in life, you are interested in almost everything and yet deeply attached to almost nothing. Everyone you know thinks that you are a little 'odd', but you probably don't mind them believing this because you know it to be true. In fact it is possible that you positively relish your eccentricity, which sets you apart from the common herd and means that you are always going to be noticed.

Although it may seem strange with this combination of Air and Fire, you can be distinctly cool on occasions, have a deep and abiding love of your own company now and again, and won't easily be understood. Love comes fairly easily to you but there are times when you are accused of being self-possessed, self-indulgent and not willing enough to fall in line with the wishes of those around you. Despite this you walk on and on down your own path. At heart you are an extrovert and you love to party, often late into the night. Luxury appeals to you, though it tends to be of the transient sort. Travel could easily play a major and a very important part in your life.

Sagittarius with Pisces Ascendant

A very attractive combination this, because the more dominant qualities of the Archer are somehow mellowed-out by the caring Water-sign qualities of the Fishes. You can be very outgoing, but there is always a deeper side to your nature that allows others to know that you are thinking about them. Few people could fall out with either your basic nature or your attitude to the world at large, even though there are depths to your personality that may not be easily understood. You are capable, have a good executive ability and can work hard to achieve your objectives, even if you get a little disillusioned on the way. Much of your life is given over to helping those around you and there is a great tendency for you to work for and on behalf of humanity as a whole. A sense of community is brought to most of what you do and you enjoy co-operation.

Although you have the natural Sagittarian ability to attract people to you, the Pisces half of your nature makes you just a little more reserved in personal matters than might otherwise be the case. More careful in your choices than either sign taken alone, you still have to make certain that your motivations when commencing a personal relationship are the right ones. You love to be happy, and to offer gifts of happiness to others.

Sagittarius with Aries Ascendant

What a lovely combination this can be, for the devil-may-care aspects of Sagittarius lighten the load of a sometimes too serious Aries interior. Everything that glistens is not gold, though it's hard to convince you of the fact because, to mix metaphors, you can make a silk purse out of a sow's ear. Almost everyone loves you, and in return you offer a friendship that is warm and protective, but not as demanding as sometimes tends to be the case with the Aries type. Relationships may be many and varied and there is often more than one major attachment in the life of those holding this combination. You can bring a breath of spring to any relationship, though you need to ensure that the person concerned is capable of keeping up with the hectic pace of your life.

It may appear from time to time that you are rather too trusting for your own good, though deep inside you are very astute, and it seems that almost everything you undertake works out well in the end. This has nothing to do with native luck and is really down to the fact that you are much more calculating than might appear to be the case at first sight. As a parent you are protective, yet offer sufficient room for self-expression.

Sagittarius with Taurus Ascendant

A dual nature is evident here, and if it doesn't serve to confuse you it will certainly be a cause of concern to many of the people with whom you share your life. You like to have a good time and are a natural party-goer. On such occasions you are accommodating, chatty and good to know. But contrast this with the quieter side of Taurus, which is directly opposed to your Sagittarian qualities. The opposition of forces is easy for you to deal with because you inhabit your own body and mind all the time, but it's far less easy for friends and relatives to understand. As a result, on those occasions when you decide that, socially speaking, enough is enough, you will need to explain the fact to the twelve people who are waiting outside your door with party hats and whoopee cushions.

Confidence to do almost anything is not far from the forefront of your mind and you readily embark on adventures that would have some types flapping about in horror. Here again, it is important to realise that we are not all built the same way and that gentle coaxing is sometimes necessary to bring others round to your point of view. If you really have a fault, it could be that you are so busy being your own, rather less than predictable self, that you fail to take the rest of the world into account.

Sagittarius with Gemini Ascendant

'Tomorrow is another day!' This is your belief and you stick to it. There isn't a brighter and more optimistic soul to be found than you and almost everyone you come into contact with is touched by the fact. Dashing about from one place to another, you manage to get more things done in one day than most other people would achieve in a week. Of course this explains why you are so likely to wear yourself out and it means that frequent periods of absolute rest are necessary if you are to remain truly healthy and happy. Sagittarius makes you brave and sometimes a little headstrong, so you need to curb your natural enthusiasm while you stop to think about the consequences of your actions.

It's not really certain if you do 'think' in the accepted sense of the word, because the lightning qualities of both these signs mean that your reactions are second to none. However, you are not indestructible and you put far more pressure on yourself than would often be sensible. Routines are not your thing at all, and many of you manage to hold down two or more jobs at once. It might be an idea to stop and smell the flowers on the way, and you could certainly do with putting your feet up much more than you do. However, you probably won't still be reading this passage because you will have something far more important to do!

Sagittarius with Cancer Ascendant

You have far more drive, enthusiasm and get-up-and-go than would seem to be the case for Cancer when taken alone, but all of this is tempered with a certain quiet compassion that probably makes you the best sort of Sagittarian too. It's true that you don't like to be on your own or to retire in your shell quite as much as the Crab usually does, though there are, even in your case, occasions when this is going to be necessary. Absolute concentration can sometimes be a problem to you, though this is hardly likely to be the case when you are dealing with matters relating to your home or family, both of which reign supreme in your thinking. Always loving and kind, you are a social animal and enjoy being out there in the real world, expressing the deeper opinions of Cancer much more readily than would often be the case with other combinations relating to the sign of the Crab.

Personality is not lacking and you tend to be very popular, not least because you are the fountain of good and practical advice. You want to get things done and retain a practical approach to most situations which is the envy of many other people. As a parent you are second to none, combining common sense, dignity and a sensible approach. To balance this you stay young enough to understand children.

Sagittarius with Leo Ascendant

Above and beyond anything else you are naturally funny, and this is an aspect of your nature that will bring you intact through a whole series of problems that you manage to create for yourself. Chatty, witty, charming, kind and loving, you personify the best qualities of both these signs, whilst also retaining the Fire-sign ability to keep going, long after the rest of the party has gone home to bed. Being great fun to have around, you attract friends in the way that a magnet attracts iron filings. Many of these will be casual connections but there will always be a nucleus of deep, abiding attachments that may stay around you for most of your life.

You don't often suffer from fatigue, but on those occasions when you do there is ample reason to stay still for a while and to take stock of situations. Routines are not your thing and you like to fill your life with variety. It's important to do certain things right, however, and staying power is something that comes with age, assisted by the Fixed quality of Leo. Few would lock horns with you in an argument, which you always have to win. In a way you are a natural debator but you can sometimes carry things too far if you are up against a worthy opponent. You have the confidence to sail through situations that would defeat others.

Sagittarius with Virgo Ascendant

This is a combination that might look rather odd at first sight because these two signs have so very little in common. However, the saying goes that opposites attract, and in terms of the personality you display to the world this is especially true in your case. Not everyone understands what makes you tick but you try to show the least complicated face to the world that you can manage to display. You can be deep and secretive on occasions, and yet at other times you can start talking as soon as you climb out of bed and never stop until you are back there again. Inspirational and spontaneous, you take the world by storm on those occasions when you are free from worries and firing on all cylinders. It is a fact that you support your friends, though there are rather more of them than would be the case for Virgo taken on its own, and you don't always choose them as wisely as you might.

There are times when you display a temper, and although Sagittarius is incapable of bearing a grudge, the same cannot be said for Virgo, which has a better memory than the elephant. For the best results in life you need to relax as much as possible and avoid overheating that powerful and busy brain. Virgo gives you the ability to concentrate on one thing at once, a skill you should encourage.

Sagittarius with Libra Ascendant

A very happy combination this, with a great desire for life in all its forms and a need to push forward the bounds of the possible in a way that few other zodiac sign connections would do. You don't like the unpleasant or ugly in life and yet you are capable of dealing with both if you have to. Giving so much to humanity, you still manage to retain a degree of individuality that would surprise many, charm others, and please all.

On the reverse side of the same coin you might find that you are sometimes accused of being fickle, but this is only an expression of your need for change and variety, which is intrinsic to both these signs. True, you have more of a temper than would be the case for Libra when taken on its own, but such incidents would see you up and down in a flash and it is almost impossible for you to bear a grudge of any sort. Routines get on your nerves and you are far happier when you can please yourself and get ahead at your own pace, which is quite fast.

As a lover you can make a big impression and most of you will not go short of affection in the early days, before you choose to commit yourself. Once you do, there is always a chance of romantic problems, but these are less likely when you have chosen carefully in the first place.

Sagittarius with Scorpio Ascendant

There are many gains with this combination, and most of you reading this will already be familiar with the majority of them. Sagittarius offers a bright and hopeful approach to life, but may not always have the staying power and the patience to get what it really needs. Scorpio, on the other hand, can be too deep for its own good, is very self-seeking on occasions and extremely giving to others. Both the signs have problems when taken on their own, and, it has to be said, double the difficulties when they come together. But this is not usually the case. Invariably the presence of Scorpio slows down the over-quick responses of the Archer, whilst the inclusion of Sagittarius prevents Scorpio from taking itself too seriously.

Life is so often a game of extremes, when all the great spiritual masters of humanity have indicated that a 'middle way' is the path to choose. You have just the right combination of skills and mental faculties to find that elusive path, and can bring great joy to yourself and others as a result. Most of the time you are happy, optimistic, helpful and a joy to know. You have mental agility, backed up by a stunning intuition, which itself would rarely let you down. Keep a sense of proportion and understand that your depth of intellect is necessary in order to curb the more flighty aspects of Scorpio.

THE MOON AND THE PART IT PLAYS IN YOUR LIFE

In astrology the Moon is probably the single most important heavenly body after the Sun. Its unique position, as partner to the Earth on its journey around the solar system, means that the Moon appears to pass through the signs of the zodiac extremely quickly. The zodiac position of the Moon at the time of your birth plays a great part in personal character and is especially significant in the build-up of your emotional nature.

Your Own Moon Sign

Discovering the position of the Moon at the time of your birth has always been notoriously difficult because tracking the complex zodiac positions of the Moon is not easy. This process has been reduced to three simple stages with our Lunar Tables. A breakdown of the Moon's zodiac positions can be found from page 35 onwards, so that once you know what your Moon Sign is, you can see what part this plays in the overall build-up of your personal character.

If you follow the instructions on the next page you will soon be able to work out exactly what zodiac sign the Moon occupied on the day that you were born and you can then go on to compare the reading for this position with those of your Sun sign and your Ascendant. It is partly the comparison between these three important positions that goes towards making you the unique individual you are.

HOW TO DISCOVER YOUR MOON SIGN

This is a three-stage process. You may need a pen and a piece of paper but if you follow the instructions below the process should only take a minute or so.

STAGE 1 First of all you need to know the Moon Age at the time of your birth. If you look at Moon Table 1, on page 33, you will find all the years between 1909 and 2007 down the left side. Find the year of your birth and then trace across to the right to the month of your birth. Where the two intersect you will find a number. This is the date of the New Moon in the month that you were born. You now need to count forward the number of days between the New Moon and your own birthday. For example, if the New Moon in the month of your birth was shown as being the 6th and you were born on the 20th, your Moon Age Day would be 14. If the New Moon in the month of your birth came after your birthday, you need to count forward from the New Moon in the previous month. If you were born in a Leap Year, remember to count the 29th February. You can tell if your birth year was a Leap Year if the last two digits can be divided by four. Whatever the result, jot this number down so that you do not forget it.

STAGE 2 Take a look at Moon Table 2 on page 34. Down the left hand column look for the date of your birth. Now trace across to the month of your birth. Where the two meet you will find a letter. Copy this letter down alongside your Moon Age Day.

STAGE 3 Moon Table 3 on page 34 will supply you with the zodiac sign the Moon occupied on the day of your birth. Look for your Moon Age Day down the left hand column and then for the letter you found in Stage 2. Where the two converge you will find a zodiac sign and this is the sign occupied by the Moon on the day that you were born.

Your Zodiac Moon Sign Explained

You will find a profile of all zodiac Moon Signs on pages 35 to 38, showing in yet another way how astrology helps to make you into the individual that you are. In each daily entry of the Astral Diary you can find the zodiac position of the Moon for every day of the year. This also allows you to discover your lunar birthdays. Since the Moon passes through all the signs of the zodiac in about a month, you can expect something like twelve lunar birthdays each year. At these times you are likely to be emotionally steady and able to make the sort of decisions that have real, lasting value.

MOON TABLE 1

YEAR	OCT	NOV	DEC	YEAR	OCT	NOV	DEC	YEAR	OCT	NOV	DEC
1909	14	13	12	1942	10	8	8	1975	5	3	3
1910	2	1	1/30	1943	29	27	27	1976	23	21	21
1911	21	20	20	1944	17	15	15	1977	12	11	10
1912	11	9	9	1945	6	4	4	1978	2/31	30	29
1913	29	28	27	1946	24	23	23	1979	20	19	18
1914	19	17	17	1947	14	12	12	1980	9	8	7
1915	8	7	6	1948	2	1	1/30	1981	27	26	26
1916	27	26	25	1949	21	20	19	1982	17	15	15
1917	15	14	13	1950	11	9	9	1983	6	4	4
1918	4	3	2	1951	1/30	29	28	1984	24	22	22
1919	23	22	21	1952	18	17	17	1985	14	12	12
1920	12	10	10	1953	8	6	6	1986	3	2	1/30
1921	1/30	29	29	1954	26	25	25	1987	22	21	20
1922	20	19	18	1955	15	14	14	1988	10	9	9
1923	10	8	8	1956	4	2	2	1989	29	28	28
1924	28	26	26	1957	23	21	21	1990	18	17	17
1925	17	16	15	1958	12	11	10	1991	8	6	6
1926	6	5	5	1959	2/31	30	29	1992	25	24	24
1927	25	24	24	1960	20	19	18	1993	15	14	14
1928	14	12	12	1961	9	8	7	1994	5	3	2
1929	2	1	1/30	1962	28	27	26	1995	24	22	22
1930	20	19	19	1963	17	15	15	1996	11	10	10
1931	11	9	9	1964	5	4	4	1997	31	30	29
1932	29	27	27	1965	24	22	22	1998	20	19	18
1933	19	17	17	1966	14	12	12	1999	8	8	7
1934	8	7	6	1967	3	2	1/30	2000	27	26	25
1935	27	26	25	1968	22	21	20	2001	17	16	15
1936	15	14	13	1969	10	9	9	2002	6	4	4
1937	4	3	2	1970	1/30	29	28	2003	25	24	23
1938	23	22	21	1971	19	18	17	2004	12	11	11
1939	12	11	10	1972	8	6	6	2005	2	1	1/31
1940	1/30	29	28	1973	26	25	25	2006	21	20	20
1941	20	19	18	1974	15	14	14	2007	11	9	9

TABLE 2   *MOON TABLE 3*

DAY	NOV	DEC	M/D	e	f	g	i	m	n	q
1	e	i	0	SC	SC	SC	SA	SA	SA	CP
2	e	i	1	SC	SC	SA	SA	SA	CP	CP
3	e	m	2	SC	SA	SA	CP	CP	CP	AQ
4	f	m	3	SA	SA	CP	CP	CP	AQ	AQ
5	f	n	4	SA	CP	CP	CP	AQ	AQ	PI
6	f	n	5	CP	CP	AQ	AQ	AQ	PI	PI
7	f	n	6	CP	AQ	AQ	AQ	AQ	PI	AR
8	f	n	7	AQ	AQ	PI	PI	PI	AR	AR
9	f	n	8	AQ	PI	PI	PI	PI	AR	AR
10	f	n	9	AQ	PI	PI	AR	AR	TA	TA
11	f	n	10	PI	AR	AR	AR	AR	TA	TA
12	f	n	11	PI	AR	AR	TA	TA	TA	GE
13	g	n	12	AR	TA	TA	TA	TA	GE	GE
14	g	n	13	AR	TA	TA	GE	GE	GE	GE
15	g	n	14	TA	GE	GE	GE	GE	CA	CA
16	g	n	15	TA	TA	TA	GE	GE	GE	CA
17	g	n	16	TA	GE	GE	GE	CA	CA	CA
18	g	n	17	GE	GE	GE	CA	CA	CA	LE
19	g	n	18	GE	GE	CA	CA	CA	LE	LE
20	g	n	19	GE	CA	CA	CA	LE	LE	LE
21	g	n	20	CA	CA	CA	LE	LE	LE	VI
22	g	n	21	CA	CA	LE	LE	LE	VI	VI
23	i	q	22	CA	LE	LE	VI	VI	VI	LI
24	i	q	23	LE	LE	LE	VI	VI	VI	LI
25	i	q	24	LE	LE	VI	VI	VI	LI	LI
26	i	q	25	LE	VI	VI	LI	LI	LI	SC
27	i	q	26	VI	VI	LI	LI	LI	SC	SC
28	i	q	27	VI	LI	LI	SC	SC	SC	SA
29	i	q	28	LI	LI	LI	SC	SC	SC	SA
30	i	q	29	LI	LI	SC	SC	SA	SA	SA
31	–	q								

AR = Aries, TA = Taurus, GE = Gemini, CA = Cancer, LE = Leo, VI = Virgo, LI = Libra, SC = Scorpio, SA = Sagittarius, CP = Capricorn, AQ = Aquarius, PI = Pisces

MOON SIGNS

Moon in Aries

You have a strong imagination, courage, determination and a desire to do things in your own way and forge your own path through life.

Originality is a key attribute; you are seldom stuck for ideas although your mind is changeable and you could take the time to focus on individual tasks. Often quick-tempered, you take orders from few people and live life at a fast pace. Avoid health problems by taking regular time out for rest and relaxation.

Emotionally, it is important that you talk to those you are closest to and work out your true feelings. Once you discover that people are there to help, there is less necessity for you to do everything yourself.

Moon in Taurus

The Moon in Taurus gives you a courteous and friendly manner, which means you are likely to have many friends.

The good things in life mean a lot to you, as Taurus is an Earth sign that delights in experiences which please the senses. Hence you are probably a lover of good food and drink, which may in turn mean you need to keep an eye on the bathroom scales, especially as looking good is also important to you.

Emotionally you are fairly stable and you stick by your own standards. Taureans do not respond well to change. Intuition also plays an important part in your life.

Moon in Gemini

You have a warm-hearted character, sympathetic and eager to help others. At times reserved, you can also be articulate and chatty: this is part of the paradox of Gemini, which always brings duplicity to the nature. You are interested in current affairs, have a good intellect, and are good company and likely to have many friends. Most of your friends have a high opinion of you and would be ready to defend you should the need arise. However, this is usually unnecessary, as you are quite capable of defending yourself in any verbal confrontation.

Travel is important to your inquisitive mind and you find intellectual stimulus in mixing with people from different cultures. You also gain much from reading, writing and the arts but you do need plenty of rest and relaxation in order to avoid fatigue.

Moon in Cancer

The Moon in Cancer at the time of birth is a fortunate position as Cancer is the Moon's natural home. This means that the qualities of compassion and understanding given by the Moon are especially enhanced in your nature, and you are friendly and sociable and cope well with emotional pressures. You cherish home and family life, and happily do the domestic tasks. Your surroundings are important to you and you hate squalor and filth. You are likely to have a love of music and poetry.

Your basic character, although at times changeable like the Moon itself, depends on symmetry. You aim to make your surroundings comfortable and harmonious, for yourself and those close to you.

Moon in Leo

The best qualities of the Moon and Leo come together to make you warm-hearted, fair, ambitious and self-confident. With good organisational abilities, you invariably rise to a position of responsibility in your chosen career. This is fortunate as you don't enjoy being an 'also-ran' and would rather be an important part of a small organisation than a menial in a large one.

You should be lucky in love, and happy, provided you put in the effort to make a comfortable home for yourself and those close to you. It is likely that you will have a love of pleasure, sport, music and literature. Life brings you many rewards, most of them as a direct result of your own efforts, although you may be luckier than average and ready to make the best of any situation.

Moon in Virgo

You are endowed with good mental abilities and a keen receptive memory, but you are never ostentatious or pretentious. Naturally quite reserved, you still have many friends, especially of the opposite sex. Marital relationships must be discussed carefully and worked at so that they remain harmonious, as personal attachments can be a problem if you do not give them your full attention.

Talented and persevering, you possess artistic qualities and are a good homemaker. Earning your honours through genuine merit, you work long and hard towards your objectives but show little pride in your achievements. Many short journeys will be undertaken in your life.

Moon in Libra

With the Moon in Libra you are naturally popular and make friends easily. People like you, probably more than you realise, you bring fun to a party and are a natural diplomat. For all its good points, Libra is not the most stable of astrological signs and, as a result, your emotions can be a little unstable too. Therefore, although the Moon in Libra is said to be good for love and marriage, your Sun sign and Rising sign will have an important effect on your emotional and loving qualities.

You must remember to relate to others in your decision-making. Co-operation is crucial because Libra represents the 'balance' of life that can only be achieved through harmonious relationships. Conformity is not easy for you because Libra, an Air sign, likes its independence.

Moon in Scorpio

Some people might call you pushy. In fact, all you really want to do is to live life to the full and protect yourself and your family from the pressures of life. Take care to avoid giving the impression of being sarcastic or impulsive and use your energies wisely and constructively.

You have great courage and you invariably achieve your goals by force of personality and sheer effort. You are fond of mystery and are good at predicting the outcome of situations and events. Travel experiences can be beneficial to you.

You may experience problems if you do not take time to examine your motives in a relationship, and also if you allow jealousy, always a feature of Scorpio, to cloud your judgement.

Moon in Sagittarius

The Moon in Sagittarius helps to make you a generous individual with humanitarian qualities and a kind heart. Restlessness may be intrinsic as your mind is seldom still. Perhaps because of this, you have a need for change that could lead you to several major moves during your adult life. You are not afraid to stand your ground when you know your judgement is right, you speak directly and have good intuition.

At work you are quick, efficient and versatile and so you make an ideal employee. You need work to be intellectually demanding and do not enjoy tedious routines.

In relationships, you anger quickly if faced with stupidity or deception, though you are just as quick to forgive and forget. Emotionally, there are times when your heart rules your head.

Moon in Capricorn

The Moon in Capricorn makes you popular and likely to come into the public eye in some way. The watery Moon is not entirely comfortable in the Earth sign of Capricorn and this may lead to some difficulties in the early years of life. An initial lack of creative ability and indecision must be overcome before the true qualities of patience and perseverance inherent in Capricorn can show through.

You have good administrative ability and are a capable worker, and if you are careful you can accumulate wealth. But you must be cautious and take professional advice in partnerships, as you are open to deception. You may be interested in social or welfare work, which suit your organisational skills and sympathy for others.

Moon in Aquarius

The Moon in Aquarius makes you an active and agreeable person with a friendly, easy-going nature. Sympathetic to the needs of others, you flourish in a laid-back atmosphere. You are broad-minded, fair and open to suggestion, although sometimes you have an unconventional quality which others can find hard to understand.

You are interested in the strange and curious, and in old articles and places. You enjoy trips to these places and gain much from them. Political, scientific and educational work interests you and you might choose a career in science or technology.

Money-wise, you make gains through innovation and concentration and Lunar Aquarians often tackle more than one job at a time. In love you are kind and honest.

Moon in Pisces

You have a kind, sympathetic nature, somewhat retiring at times, but you always take account of others' feelings and help when you can.

Personal relationships may be problematic, but as life goes on you can learn from your experiences and develop a better understanding of yourself and the world around you.

You have a fondness for travel, appreciate beauty and harmony and hate disorder and strife. You may be fond of literature and would make a good writer or speaker yourself. You have a creative imagination and may come across as an incurable romantic. You have strong intuition, maybe bordering on a mediumistic quality, which sets you apart from the mass. You may not be rich in cash terms, but your personal gifts are worth more than gold.

SAGITTARIUS IN LOVE

Discover how compatible in love you are with people from the same and other signs of the zodiac. Five stars equals a match made in heaven!

Sagittarius meets Sagittarius

Although perhaps not the very best partnership for Sagittarius, this must rank as one of the most eventful, electrifying and interesting of the bunch. They will think alike, which is often the key to any relationship but, unfortunately, they may be so busy leading their own lives that they don't spend much time together. Their social life should be something special, and there could be lots of travel. However, domestic responsibilities need to be carefully shared and the family might benefit from a helping hand in this area. Star rating: ****

Sagittarius meets Capricorn

Any real problem here will stem from a lack of understanding. Capricorn is very practical and needs to be constantly on the go, though in a fairly low-key sort of way. Sagittarius is busy too, though always in a panic and invariably behind its deadlines, which will annoy organised Capricorn. Sagittarius doesn't really have the depth of nature that best suits an Earth sign like Capricorn and its flirty nature could upset the sensitive Goat, though its lighter attitude could be cheering, too. Star rating: ***

Sagittarius meets Aquarius

Both Sagittarius and Aquarius are into mind games, which may lead to something of an intellectual competition. If one side is happy to be bamboozled it won't be a problem, but it is more likely that the relationship will turn into a competition which won't auger well for its long-term future. However, on the plus side, both signs are adventurous and sociable, so as long as there is always something new and interesting to do, the match could end up turning out very well. Star rating: **

Sagittarius meets Pisces

Probably the least likely success story for either sign, which is why it scores so low on the star rating. The basic problem is an almost total lack of understanding. A successful relationship needs empathy and progress towards a shared goal but, although both are eager to please, Pisces is too deep and Sagittarius too flighty – they just don't belong on the same planet! As pals, they have more in common and so a friendship is the best hope of success and happiness. Star rating: *

Sagittarius meets Aries

This can be one of the most favourable matches of them all. Both Aries and Sagittarius are Fire signs, which often leads to clashes of will, but this pair find a mutual understanding. Sagittarius helps Aries to develop a better sense of humour, while Aries teaches the Archer about consistency on the road to success. Some patience is called for on both sides, but these people have a natural liking for each other. Add this to growing love and you have a long-lasting combination that is hard to beat. Star rating: *****

Sagittarius meets Taurus

On first impression, Taurus may not like Sagittarius, which may seem brash, and even common, when viewed through the Bull's refined eyes. But, there is hope of success because the two signs have so much to offer each other. The Archer is enthralled by the Taurean's natural poise and beauty, while Taurus always needs more basic confidence, which is no problem to Sagittarius who has plenty to spare. Both signs love to travel. There are certain to be ups and downs, but that doesn't prevent an interesting, inspiring and even exciting combination. Star rating: ***

Sagittarius meets Gemini

A paradoxical relationship this. On paper, the two signs have much in common, but unfortunately, they are often so alike that life turns into a fiercely fought competition. Both signs love change and diversity and both want to be the life and soul of the party. But in life there must always be a leader and a follower, and neither of this pair wants to be second. Both also share a tendency towards infidelity, which may develop into a problem as time passes. This could be an interesting match, but not necessarily successful. Star rating: **

Sagittarius meets Cancer

Although probably not an immediate success, there is hope for this couple. It's hard to see how this pair could get together, because they have few mutual interests. Sagittarius is always on the go, loves a hectic social life and dances the night away. Cancer prefers the cinema or a concert. But, having met, Cancer will appreciate the Archer's happy and cheerful nature, while Sagittarius finds Cancer alluring and intriguing and, as the saying goes, opposites attract. A long-term relationship would focus on commitment to family, with Cancer leading this area. Star rating: ***

Sagittarius meets Leo

An excellent match as Leo and Sagittarius have so much in common. Their general approach to life is very similar, although as they are both Fire signs they can clash impressively! Sagittarius is shallower and more flippant than Leo likes to think of itself, and the Archer will be the one taking emotional chances. Sagittarius has met its match in the Lion's den, as brave Leo won't be outdone by anyone. Financially, they will either be very wealthy or struggling, and family life may be chaotic. Problems, like joys, are handled jointly – and that leads to happiness. Star rating: *****

Sagittarius meets Virgo

There can be some quite strange happenings inside this relationship. Sagittarius and Virgo view life so differently there are always new discoveries. Virgo is much more of a home-bird than Sagittarius, but that won't matter if the Archer introduces its hectic social life gradually. More importantly, Sagittarius understands that it takes Virgo a long time to free its hidden 'inner sprite', but once free it will be fun all the way – until Virgo's thrifty nature takes over. There are great possibilities, but effort is required. Star rating: ***

Sagittarius meets Libra

Libra and Sagittarius are both adaptable signs who get on well with most people, but this promising outlook often does not follow through because each brings out the 'flighty' side of the other. This combination is great for a fling, but when the romance is over someone needs to see to the practical side of life. Both signs are well meaning, pleasant and kind, but are either of them constant enough to build a life together? In at least some cases, the answer would be no. Star rating: ***

Sagittarius meets Scorpio

Sagittarius needs constant stimulation and loves to be busy from dawn till dusk which may mean that it feels rather frustrated by Scorpio. Scorpions are hard workers, too, but they are also contemplative and need periods of quiet which may mean that they appear dull to Sagittarius. This could lead to a gulf between the two which must be overcome. With time and patience on both sides, this can be a lucrative encounter and good in terms of home and family. A variable alliance. Star rating: ***

VENUS:
THE PLANET OF LOVE

If you look up at the sky around sunset or sunrise you will often see Venus in close attendance to the Sun. It is arguably one of the most beautiful sights of all and there is little wonder that historically it became associated with the goddess of love. But although Venus does play an important part in the way you view love and in the way others see you romantically, this is only one of the spheres of influence that it enjoys in your overall character.

Venus has a part to play in the more cultured side of your life and has much to do with your appreciation of art, literature, music and general creativity. Even the way you look is responsive to the part of the zodiac that Venus occupied at the start of your life, though this fact is also down to your Sun sign and Ascending sign. If, at the time you were born, Venus occupied one of the more gregarious zodiac signs, you will be more likely to wear your heart on your sleeve, as well as to be more attracted to entertainment, social gatherings and good company. If on the other hand Venus occupied a quiet zodiac sign at the time of your birth, you would tend to be more retiring and less willing to shine in public situations.

It's good to know what part the planet Venus plays in your life for it can have a great bearing on the way you appear to the rest of the world and since we all have to mix with others, you can learn to make the very best of what Venus has to offer you.

One of the great complications in the past has always been trying to establish exactly what zodiac position Venus enjoyed when you were born because the planet is notoriously difficult to track. However, we have solved that problem by creating a table that is exclusive to your Sun sign, which you will find on the following page.

Establishing your Venus sign could not be easier. Just look up the year of your birth on the following page and you will see a sign of the zodiac. This was the sign that Venus occupied in the period covered by your sign in that year. If Venus occupied more than one sign during the period, this is indicated by the date on which the sign changed, and the name of the new sign. For instance, if you were born in 1950, Venus was in Sagittarius until the 16th December, after which time it was in Capricorn. If you were born before 16th December your Venus sign is Sagittarius, if you were born on or after 16th December, your Venus sign is Capricorn. Once you have established the position of Venus at the time of your birth, you can then look in the pages which follow to see how this has a bearing on your life as a whole.

1909 CAPRICORN / 6.12 AQUARIUS
1910 SCORPIO / 24.11 SAGITTARIUS /
18.12 CAPRICORN
1911 LIBRA / 8.12 SCORPIO
1912 CAPRICORN / 13.12 AQUARIUS
1913 SCORPIO / 8.12 SAGITTARIUS
1914 SAGITTARIUS / 6.12 SCORPIO
1915 SAGITTARIUS / 3.12 CAPRICORN
1916 LIBRA / 27.11 SCORPIO
1917 CAPRICORN / 6.12 AQUARIUS
1918 SAGITTARIUS / 18.12 CAPRICORN
1919 LIBRA / 9.12 SCORPIO
1920 CAPRICORN / 13.12 AQUARIUS
1921 SCORPIO / 7.12 SAGITTARIUS
1922 SAGITTARIUS / 29.11 SCORPIO
1923 SAGITTARIUS / 2.12 CAPRICORN
1924 LIBRA / 27.11 SCORPIO
1925 CAPRICORN / 6.12 AQUARIUS
1926 SAGITTARIUS / 17.12 CAPRICORN
1927 LIBRA / 9.12 SCORPIO
1928 CAPRICORN / 13.12 AQUARIUS
1929 SCORPIO / 7.12 SAGITTARIUS
1930 SCORPIO
1931 SAGITTARIUS / 2.12 CAPRICORN
1932 LIBRA / 26.11 SCORPIO
1933 CAPRICORN / 6.12 AQUARIUS
1934 SAGITTARIUS / 17.12 CAPRICORN
1935 LIBRA / 10.12 SCORPIO
1936 CAPRICORN / 12.12 AQUARIUS
1937 SCORPIO / 6.12 SAGITTARIUS
1938 SCORPIO
1939 SAGITTARIUS / 1.12 CAPRICORN
1940 LIBRA / 26.11 SCORPIO
1941 CAPRICORN / 6.12 AQUARIUS
1942 SAGITTARIUS / 16.12 CAPRICORN
1943 LIBRA / 10.12 SCORPIO
1944 CAPRICORN / 12.12 AQUARIUS
1945 SCORPIO / 6.12 SAGITTARIUS
1946 SCORPIO
1947 SAGITTARIUS / 1.12 CAPRICORN
1948 LIBRA / 25.11 SCORPIO /
20.12 SAGITTARIUS
1949 CAPRICORN / 7.12 AQUARIUS
1950 SAGITTARIUS / 16.12 CAPRICORN
1951 LIBRA / 10.12 SCORPIO
1952 CAPRICORN / 11.12 AQUARIUS
1953 SCORPIO / 5.12 SAGITTARIUS
1954 SCORPIO
1955 SAGITTARIUS / 30.11 CAPRICORN
1956 LIBRA / 25.11 SCORPIO /
20.12 SAGITTARIUS
1957 CAPRICORN / 8.12 AQUARIUS

1958 SAGITTARIUS / 15.12 CAPRICORN
1959 LIBRA / 10.12 SCORPIO
1960 CAPRICORN / 11.12 AQUARIUS
1961 SCORPIO / 5.12 SAGITTARIUS
1962 SCORPIO
1963 SAGITTARIUS / 30.11 CAPRICORN
1964 LIBRA / 24.11 SCORPIO /
19.12 SAGITTARIUS
1965 CAPRICORN / 8.12 AQUARIUS
1966 SAGITTARIUS / 15.12 CAPRICORN
1967 LIBRA / 10.12 SCORPIO
1968 CAPRICORN / 10.12 AQUARIUS
1969 SCORPIO / 4.12 SAGITTARIUS
1970 SCORPIO
1971 SAGITTARIUS / 29.11 CAPRICORN
1972 LIBRA / 24.11 SCORPIO /
19.12 SAGITTARIUS
1973 CAPRICORN / 9.12 AQUARIUS
1974 SAGITTARIUS / 14.12 CAPRICORN
1975 LIBRA / 9.12 SCORPIO
1976 CAPRICORN / 9.12 AQUARIUS
1977 SCORPIO / 4.12 SAGITTARIUS
1978 SCORPIO
1979 SAGITTARIUS / 28.11 CAPRICORN
1980 SCORPIO / 18.12 SAGITTARIUS
1981 CAPRICORN / 10.12 AQUARIUS
1982 SAGITTARIUS / 14.12 CAPRICORN
1983 LIBRA / 9.12 SCORPIO
1984 CAPRICORN / 9.12 AQUARIUS
1985 SCORPIO / 3.12 SAGITTARIUS
1986 SCORPIO
1987 SAGITTARIUS / 28.11 CAPRICORN
1988 SCORPIO / 18.12 SAGITTARIUS
1989 CAPRICORN / 11.12 AQUARIUS
1990 SAGITTARIUS / 13.12 CAPRICORN
1991 LIBRA / 9.12 SCORPIO
1992 CAPRICORN / 9.12 AQUARIUS
1993 SCORPIO / 3.12 SAGITTARIUS
1994 SCORPIO
1995 SAGITTARIUS / 28.11 CAPRICORN
1996 SCORPIO / 17.12 SAGITTARIUS
1997 CAPRICORN / 12.12 AQUARIUS
1998 SAGITTARIUS / 13.12 CAPRICORN
1999 LIBRA / 9.12 SCORPIO
2000 CAPRICORN / 8.12 AQUARIUS
2001 SCORPIO / 3.12 SAGITTARIUS
2002 SCORPIO
2003 SAGITTARIUS/28.11 CAPRICORN
2004 SCORPIO / 17.12 SAGITTARIUS
2005 CAPRICORN / 12.12 AQUARIUS
2006 SAGITTARIUS / 13.12 CAPRICORN
2007 LIBRA / 9.12 SCORPIO

VENUS THROUGH THE ZODIAC SIGNS

Venus in Aries

Amongst other things, the position of Venus in Aries indicates a fondness for travel, music and all creative pursuits. Your nature tends to be affectionate and you would try not to create confusion or difficulty for others if it could be avoided. Many people with this planetary position have a great love of the theatre, and mental stimulation is of the greatest importance. Early romantic attachments are common with Venus in Aries, so it is very important to establish a genuine sense of romantic continuity. Early marriage is not recommended, especially if it is based on sympathy. You may give your heart a little too readily on occasions.

Venus in Taurus

You are capable of very deep feelings and your emotions tend to last for a very long time. This makes you a trusting partner and lover, whose constancy is second to none. In life you are precise and careful and always try to do things the right way. Although this means an ordered life, which you are comfortable with, it can also lead you to be rather too fussy for your own good. Despite your pleasant nature, you are very fixed in your opinions and quite able to speak your mind. Others are attracted to you and historical astrologers always quoted this position of Venus as being very fortunate in terms of marriage. However, if you find yourself involved in a failed relationship, it could take you a long time to trust again.

Venus in Gemini

As with all associations related to Gemini, you tend to be quite versatile, anxious for change and intelligent in your dealings with the world at large. You may gain money from more than one source but you are equally good at spending it. There is an inference here that you are a good communicator, via either the written or the spoken word, and you love to be in the company of interesting people. Always on the look-out for culture, you may also be very fond of music, and love to indulge the curious and cultured side of your nature. In romance you tend to have more than one relationship and could find yourself associated with someone who has previously been a friend or even a distant relative.

Venus in Cancer

You often stay close to home because you are very fond of family and enjoy many of your most treasured moments when you are with those you love. Being naturally sympathetic, you will always do anything you can to support those around you, even people you hardly know at all. This charitable side of your nature is your most noticeable trait and is one of the reasons why others are naturally so fond of you. Being receptive and in some cases even psychic, you can see through to the soul of most of those with whom you come into contact. You may not commence too many romantic attachments but when you do give your heart, it tends to be unconditionally.

Venus in Leo

It must become quickly obvious to almost anyone you meet that you are kind, sympathetic and yet determined enough to stand up for anyone or anything that is truly important to you. Bright and sunny, you warm the world with your natural enthusiasm and would rarely do anything to hurt those around you, or at least not intentionally. In romance you are ardent and sincere, though some may find your style just a little overpowering. Gains come through your contacts with other people and this could be especially true with regard to romance, for love and money often come hand in hand for those who were born with Venus in Leo. People claim to understand you, though you are more complex than you seem.

Venus in Virgo

Your nature could well be fairly quiet no matter what your Sun sign might be, though this fact often manifests itself as an inner peace and would not prevent you from being basically sociable. Some delays and even the odd disappointment in love cannot be ruled out with this planetary position, though it's a fact that you will usually find the happiness you look for in the end. Catapulting yourself into romantic entanglements that you know to be rather ill-advised is not sensible, and it would be better to wait before you committed yourself exclusively to any one person. It is the essence of your nature to serve the world at large and through doing so it is possible that you will attract money at some stage in your life.

Venus in Libra

Venus is very comfortable in Libra and bestows upon those people who have this planetary position a particular sort of kindness that is easy to recognise. This is a very good position for all sorts of friendships and also for romantic attachments that usually bring much joy into your life. Few individuals with Venus in Libra would avoid marriage and since you are capable of great depths of love, it is likely that you will find a contented personal life. You like to mix with people of integrity and intelligence but don't take kindly to scruffy surroundings or work that means getting your hands too dirty. Careful speculation, good business dealings and money through marriage all seem fairly likely.

Venus in Scorpio

You are quite open and tend to spend money quite freely, even on those occasions when you don't have very much. Although your intentions are always good, there are times when you get yourself in to the odd scrape and this can be particularly true when it comes to romance, which you may come to late or from a rather unexpected direction. Certainly you have the power to be happy and to make others contented on the way, but you find the odd stumbling block on your journey through life and it could seem that you have to work harder than those around you. As a result of this, you gain a much deeper understanding of the true value of personal happiness than many people ever do, and are likely to achieve true contentment in the end.

Venus in Sagittarius

You are lighthearted, cheerful and always able to see the funny side of any situation. These facts enhance your popularity, which is especially high with members of the opposite sex. You should never have to look too far to find romantic interest in your life, though it is just possible that you might be too willing to commit yourself before you are certain that the person in question is right for you. Part of the problem here extends to other areas of life too. The fact is that you like variety in everything and so can tire of situations that fail to offer it. All the same, if you choose wisely and learn to understand your restless side, then great happiness can be yours.

Venus in Capricorn

The most notable trait that comes from Venus in this position is that it makes you trustworthy and able to take on all sorts of responsibilities in life. People are instinctively fond of you and love you all the more because you are always ready to help those who are in any form of need. Social and business popularity can be yours and there is a magnetic quality to your nature that is particularly attractive in a romantic sense. Anyone who wants a partner for a lover, a spouse and a good friend too would almost certainly look in your direction. Constancy is the hallmark of your nature and unfaithfulness would go right against the grain. You might sometimes be a little too trusting.

Venus in Aquarius

This location of Venus offers a fondness for travel and a desire to try out something new at every possible opportunity. You are extremely easy to get along with and tend to have many friends from varied backgrounds, classes and inclinations. You like to live a distinct sort of life and gain a great deal from moving about, both in a career sense and with regard to your home. It is not out of the question that you could form a romantic attachment to someone who comes from far away or be attracted to a person of a distinctly artistic and original nature. What you cannot stand is jealousy, for you have friends of both sexes and would want to keep things that way.

Venus in Pisces

The first thing people tend to notice about you is your wonderful, warm smile. Being very charitable by nature you will do anything to help others, even if you don't know them well. Much of your life may be spent sorting out situations for other people, but it is very important to feel that you are living for yourself too. In the main, you remain cheerful, and tend to be quite attractive to members of the opposite sex. Where romantic attachments are concerned, you could be drawn to people who are significantly older or younger than yourself or to someone with a unique career or point of view. It might be best for you to avoid marrying whilst you are still very young.

SAGITTARIUS:
2006 DIARY PAGES

 *October* 2006

1 SUNDAY
Moon Age Day 9   Moon Sign Capricorn

It would be just as well if you are not a person who works on a Sunday because the present position of the Moon can act as something of a brake on professional progress. Rather you need to concentrate on your social life, and to make sure it is interesting and stimulating today.

2 MONDAY
Moon Age Day 10   Moon Sign Aquarius

Trends assist you to reach a definite peak as far as communications generally are concerned. This is a favourable day to get your message across and to let those around you know that you are open to negotiation. Don't be held back by the odd peculiar type, because some people should be ignored at present.

3 TUESDAY
Moon Age Day 11   Moon Sign Aquarius

Socially speaking you can be on top form today and have scope to mix and mingle as much as proves to be possible. Even if some of you are up and against it at work, if you simply take things one at a time you should be able to make a significant amount of progress.

4 WEDNESDAY
Moon Age Day 12   Moon Sign Pisces

Your popularity seems to be decidedly strong at the moment and there would be no harm at all in making the most of the fact. Calling in favours would be sensible, not to mention getting those around you on board with sensational new ideas that are only just occurring to you.

5 THURSDAY   *Moon Age Day 13   Moon Sign Pisces*

An issue from the past could well resurface at any time now and this time you would be wise to deal with it properly. Don't ignore the needs of family members, especially those who seem to be very quiet at present. The attitude of your partner is also important, and they might respond well to a good chat.

6 FRIDAY   *Moon Age Day 14   Moon Sign Pisces*

There is a strong accent on leisure and pleasure as the weekend comes into view. This would be an excellent time to take an occasional day away from work and to do something that appeals but which is not important in any sort of practical sense. You need to make sure you are on top form when giving a talk or impressing others.

7 SATURDAY   *Moon Age Day 15   Moon Sign Aries*

Getting your own way with others is really not the issue this weekend but rather going with the flow. You can gain a great deal by simply accepting that those around you have opinions of their own. It wouldn't hurt at all to let someone get their own way for once, and you might even be able to gain friends as a result.

8 SUNDAY   *Moon Age Day 16   Moon Sign Aries*

You could benefit now from the good advice of a friend that comes along at a very opportune time. A day to find moments to relax, perhaps by taking a walk or getting to grips with some gardening. Don't stake your reputation on dodgy ground and leave major decisions for a day or two – whilst you simply observe life.

9 MONDAY   *Moon Age Day 17   Moon Sign Taurus*

You would be wise to let others handle major decisions today, particularly if you aren't in the mood to do so yourself. Mercury is presently in your solar twelfth house so you may not be quite as chatty as would normally be the case. At work you might decide that a brief lay-off is in order.

10 TUESDAY · *Moon Age Day 18   Moon Sign Taurus*

A slight upward turn is on offer today, but it won't last for long so make the most of it. You can elicit help from a number of directions you didn't expect, and can be quite ingenious in the way you handle the general issues of your life. Partnerships are well highlighted now.

11 WEDNESDAY · *Moon Age Day 19   Moon Sign Gemini*

With the lunar low now around you might decide not to take on anything new until the back end of the week. Your best approach is simply to stand and stare for a while and maybe get some fresh air before the cold weather begins to set in. This is not a good time to take chances of any sort.

12 THURSDAY · *Moon Age Day 20   Moon Sign Gemini*

You could easily run out of steam quite quickly at the moment and you would be wise to pace yourself carefully in order to avoid exhaustion. If the attitude of friends is difficult to understand, you might find yourself becoming easily confused. Don't worry, you can make sure that everything looks better by tomorrow.

13 FRIDAY · *Moon Age Day 21   Moon Sign Cancer*

Your emotional state can have a bearing on the decisions you are likely to be making around this time. Even if confidence is starting to grow again, for the moment you might be quite happy allowing others to make at least some of the running. Romance is highlighted for some but even there it is possible you will encounter obstacles.

14 SATURDAY · *Moon Age Day 22   Moon Sign Cancer*

Venus is now in your solar eleventh house, an influence that assists you to be the life and soul of any party that is going on in your vicinity. Relating to others should be easy and your accustomed ability to chat away ten to the dozen returns. The active and enterprising side of Sagittarius can now be put on display again.

15 SUNDAY
Moon Age Day 23   Moon Sign Leo

Among friends you tend to assert yourself willingly and with no trouble at all. Although you don't normally have a problem with strangers you could be just a little shyer than would usually be the case. Fortunately such a period is never going to last long for gregarious and intrepid Sagittarius!

16 MONDAY
Moon Age Day 24   Moon Sign Leo

This is a wonderful time for looking at social matters and for making new friends. You have scope to be bright, keen to get on with things and able to co-operate when it matters the most. If someone you haven't seen for quite some time makes a return to your life, they could well bring some interesting news with them.

17 TUESDAY
Moon Age Day 25   Moon Sign Virgo

This is a day to push towards career success. You have what it takes to get people to listen to what you have to say and to follow your lead in the main. You won't take too kindly to being told what to do but a little discretion is very important. Avoid getting on the wrong side of superiors.

18 WEDNESDAY
Moon Age Day 26   Moon Sign Virgo

Self-determination can be slightly lacking whilst Mercury remains in your solar twelfth house, and it could seem that others are failing to understand what you are telling them. It's worth making certain that you explain yourself and that you are quite definite in your views and opinions.

19 THURSDAY
Moon Age Day 27   Moon Sign Virgo

Any work that involves you in direct co-operation with others is extremely well highlighted around now. You probably won't want to go it alone in any case and can gain a great deal by being part of a team. Although the Archer sometimes tends to dominate, this isn't the case under present influences.

53

20 FRIDAY
Moon Age Day 28   Moon Sign Libra

Social life and group ventures remain central themes in your life and you are in a position to discover that you have friends you never dreamed about. What really shows out right now is how diplomatic you are capable of being. Getting what you want from life might be so easy that you barely have to try.

21 SATURDAY
Moon Age Day 0   Moon Sign Libra

The Sun now enters your solar twelfth house and although this is not an influence you should worry about, it is going to bring a potentially quieter period for the next three or four weeks, particularly in terms of your ability to communicate. Never mind, a quieter Archer can be just what is needed in order to instil confidence in others.

22 SUNDAY
Moon Age Day 1   Moon Sign Scorpio

When it comes to practical matters you should be right on the ball at the moment. You have what it takes to see clear through to the heart of just about any matter and will be able to show that penetrating insight that occasionally sets you apart. Don't be too quick to judge the actions or intentions of a friend.

23 MONDAY
Moon Age Day 2   Moon Sign Scorpio

Concentration can suffer a little today, and it is worth re-checking almost anything when it comes to important actions or decisions. You would be wise not go around blithely ignoring what others think, and in fact it would serve your purposes very well to make sure you have taken their opinions into account.

24 TUESDAY
Moon Age Day 3   Moon Sign Scorpio

It is possible that emotional aspects of your life are something you simply cannot avoid looking at today. Maybe your partner has difficulties or doesn't agree with you about certain matters. Be certain of what you are doing at work, whilst at the same time being willing to listen to an alternative point of view.

25 WEDNESDAY   *Moon Age Day 4   Moon Sign Sagittarius*

A word in the right ear might be all you need to get ahead whilst the lunar high is around. With everything to play for, only the slightly quieter quality of your present nature might get in the way. All the same, you have what it takes to ooze confidence and to persuade others to listen carefully to what you have to say.

26 THURSDAY   *Moon Age Day 5   Moon Sign Sagittarius*

This is a day during which trends assist you to get more or less what you want from life. You needn't hold back at all, and a little cheek really does go a long way. Creative potential is extremely strong but not half so noteworthy as your popularity. This is a great time to socialise.

27 FRIDAY   *Moon Age Day 6   Moon Sign Capricorn*

There seems to be no stopping you now, especially where material matters are concerned. With the weekend in view you have an opportunity to arrange gatherings of some kind and you are also in a position to show great compassion for anyone who has been having problems of one sort or another.

28 SATURDAY   ☿ *Moon Age Day 7   Moon Sign Capricorn*

Even if personal ambitions seem to be on course at present, beware of overstepping the mark and expecting too much from others. A little diplomacy goes a long way, particularly where your partner is concerned. There might be a slight tendency for you to be overdominating with certain quieter individuals.

29 SUNDAY   ☿ *Moon Age Day 8   Moon Sign Aquarius*

A personal matter might test your patience today but is unlikely to do so if you ignore it for the moment. It isn't that you are burying matters but simply waiting for a more opportune time. Some Archers will be quite happy to stay around home on this Sunday and a little genuine relaxation would probably do you good.

30 MONDAY ☿ *Moon Age Day 9   Moon Sign Aquarius*

If you feel that your love life is somewhat in the doldrums, now is the time to do something about the situation. Why not simply tell your partner just how important they are to you and maybe buy them a bunch of flowers or some other small gift? You know how much you care, but now is the time to demonstrate the fact.

31 TUESDAY ☿ *Moon Age Day 10   Moon Sign Aquarius*

It might be rather obvious now that you need to adopt a different strategy where a particular matter is concerned. Whatever this might be, just make sure you don't go over the top. Slow and steady wins most races for you at this time, and there isn't much to be gained by going at things with too much energy.

November

2006

1 WEDNESDAY ☿ *Moon Age Day 11 Moon Sign Pisces*

Personal relationships could again prove to have one or two drawbacks at the beginning of this month, and so a little reassurance can go a long way. Just as long as people know you care, you can make sure that all is well. A day to take time out to make a special fuss of any family member who is going through a hard time.

2 THURSDAY ☿ *Moon Age Day 12 Moon Sign Pisces*

Trends assist you to improve your personal life and romance could figure strongly – mainly as a result of the effort you have been putting in across the last couple of days. The time is right to allow some situations to look after themselves, especially at work, and not to control everything on your own.

3 FRIDAY ☿ *Moon Age Day 13 Moon Sign Aries*

You could discover that the creative side of your nature is predominating quite strongly now. Any new projects that find you showing these abilities suit you down to the ground. Even if you are still somewhat quieter than might normally be the case, when it matters the most you can get the message across fine.

4 SATURDAY ☿ *Moon Age Day 14 Moon Sign Aries*

You need to retreat from the world now and again and this weekend could offer the perfect opportunity to do so. There is a natural inclination to stick to those people with whom you feel most comfortable. On the way you have a chance to offer the love and support that is so much appreciated by family and close friends.

5 SUNDAY ☿ *Moon Age Day 15* *Moon Sign Taurus*

There are moments today when you might feel it is necessary to stand and fight your corner, though you could be entirely wrong in this assumption. Irritations tend to be sustained by arguing, whereas if you take a quiet and controlled approach, life is peaceful. A little outing later in the day might suit you.

6 MONDAY ☿ *Moon Age Day 16* *Moon Sign Taurus*

If the need to feel busy is uppermost in your mind at the moment, you will probably be doing something from the time you get up until the moment you crawl back into bed again. There's nothing particularly strange about that for the Archer, but you ought to find at least a few moments to meditate.

7 TUESDAY ☿ *Moon Age Day 17* *Moon Sign Gemini*

As the lunar low arrives, a social matter could cause you a few disappointments, particularly if you are expecting more from others than they are able to offer. Concentrate instead on your work, where you have scope to get on rather well. By the evening you might be quite happy to curl up in front of the television.

8 WEDNESDAY ☿ *Moon Age Day 18* *Moon Sign Gemini*

Certain obstacles could be unavoidable today but instead of concentrating on these, focus on things that are working out well instead. Be willing to take a new look at an old problem and enlist the support of family members. By doing so you should be able to make them feel important.

9 THURSDAY ☿ *Moon Age Day 19* *Moon Sign Cancer*

Progress may not resume quite the way you would wish for the next couple of days, so you might decide to take things easy. You have scope to sort out most situations if you simply wait for a while and there is plenty of assistance from specialists if you are facing something you really don't understand.

10 FRIDAY   ☿ *Moon Age Day 20   Moon Sign Cancer*

Looking for something special to do that will blow the cobwebs away and make you feel more alive? Then join the rest of the people born under your zodiac sign. One thing you do have is great compassion for other people, and that itself might be enough to keep you busy today.

11 SATURDAY   ☿ *Moon Age Day 21   Moon Sign Leo*

A better day is possible, this being a perfect time for engaging in outdoor activities. You ought to find life carefree and pleasant and can afford to stay in the company of people you find attractive and interesting. There is room to please yourself during the weekend but beware of taking too much on in a practical sense.

12 SUNDAY   ☿ *Moon Age Day 22   Moon Sign Leo*

You tend to be in a phase now during which the focus is on domestic matters. Perhaps you are securing your castle for the upcoming winter or maybe worrying about younger family members who appear to be going slightly off the rails. Treat all situations with humour and they will seem less important.

13 MONDAY   ☿ *Moon Age Day 23   Moon Sign Virgo*

Beware of taking everything you hear as being the truth today because there may be some fairly unreliable people around. You need a hefty pinch of salt and the utilisation of your own imagination and common sense. Sagittarius is still able to see the funny side of life and this in itself could turn out to be very important.

14 TUESDAY   ☿ *Moon Age Day 24   Moon Sign Virgo*

Though you might feel slightly insecure in one or two ways, in the main you can get things running fairly smoothly for you. Mercury is in your solar first house, which has to be good as far as personal and romantic trends are concerned. There may well be some interesting people around later in the day.

15 WEDNESDAY ☿   *Moon Age Day 25   Moon Sign Virgo*

The planet Venus is standing between your twelfth and first houses, and this could bring a slight lack of confidence at the very time you need it the most. Your best response is to confirm all matters before committing yourself and don't sign documents today unless you are sure you have read the small print properly.

16 THURSDAY ☿   *Moon Age Day 26   Moon Sign Libra*

Trends suggest you may spend a great deal of time today trying to please others, and despite your best efforts it won't always work. You might have to accept that there are some types who are quite happy being miserable and that there is very little you can do about it. Close friends shouldn't cause you any problems, so stick with them.

17 FRIDAY ☿   *Moon Age Day 27   Moon Sign Libra*

You could now be quite preoccupied with trying to get to the root of any matters that have been on your mind for some time. Maybe if you relaxed more you would find the answers you seek because they probably won't come along if you are worrying all the time. Never mind, much better times are available soon.

18 SATURDAY ☿   *Moon Age Day 28   Moon Sign Scorpio*

A day to take life in your stride and find time to relax in good company. It might have seemed for much of the last week that you have failed to make the progress you always expect of yourself, but it could be that things are working out better than you expected in any case. Why not try for a varied social life this weekend?

19 SUNDAY   *Moon Age Day 29   Moon Sign Scorpio*

You are often easily influenced by the prevailing social atmosphere and since this is likely to look particularly good at the moment, you can make sure that today works out well. In a day or two the Sun will move into your solar first house, but in the meantime you could feel as though you are treading water.

20 MONDAY   *Moon Age Day 0   Moon Sign Scorpio*

Beware of falling prey to the manipulative tendencies of those around you and in particular of reacting to emotional blackmail. You need to be a little hard in your dealings with others, especially if you know they are somehow taking you for a ride. Routines might seem tedious, but they can work for you right now.

21 TUESDAY   *Moon Age Day 1   Moon Sign Sagittarius*

The lunar high comes along at the same time as the Sun is moving into your solar first house so you can make the most of a couple of days that look markedly better than anything for the last week or so. A day to do what appeals to you the most and to enjoy the fact that others seem to be doing all they can to please you.

22 WEDNESDAY   *Moon Age Day 2   Moon Sign Sagittarius*

You have the ability to put yourself in the right place at the best possible time. Make the most of the fact that you can get life to go your way, and be bold in your approach to others, especially at work. Any contradictions that come along are best dealt with straight away, but you needn't let them spoil your day.

23 THURSDAY   *Moon Age Day 3   Moon Sign Capricorn*

The Sun in your first house certainly assists you to show your best side and the typical optimistic and bright Archer is now firmly on display. Keeping on top of work should be a piece of cake but what appeals to you the most is simply pleasing yourself. You can find proof of your present popularity in the actions of friends.

24 FRIDAY   *Moon Age Day 4   Moon Sign Capricorn*

Attracting life's little pleasures is facilitated by present astrological trends and you shouldn't have to work very hard in order to get others on your side. Romance looks especially good and you have what it takes to attract a great deal of affection when it matters the most.

25 SATURDAY   *Moon Age Day 5   Moon Sign Aquarius*

Recent efforts to make an impression on life are certainly not wasted and you can afford to be doing all you can to get ahead even more. In a professional sense this may not be too easy at the weekend but if you are a Saturday worker it would be sensible to put in that extra bit of effort that gets you noticed.

26 SUNDAY   *Moon Age Day 6   Moon Sign Aquarius*

Your powers of attraction are now potentially at a peak and you would be wise to make the most of the fact. It's time to call in favours and to ask for that special help that can make all the difference to something you have been planning. A day to consolidate your finances, even if you have to spend more right now.

27 MONDAY   *Moon Age Day 7   Moon Sign Aquarius*

Your sense of curiosity is much heightened by present trends and you probably want to know the ins and outs of everything. That's fine, but just remember what happened to the cat and make sure you are not treading on the sensibilities of others. Don't be too quick to judge the actions of a family member today.

28 TUESDAY   *Moon Age Day 8   Moon Sign Pisces*

This is a fantastic day to be around your favourite people. There are gains to be made on the financial front and a generally optimistic attitude should prevail. This is Sagittarius at its brightest and best and it's something that everyone likes to see. This is especially true in the case of your partner or someone you really fancy.

29 WEDNESDAY   *Moon Age Day 9   Moon Sign Pisces*

You have scope to display both the impact and sparkle of your personality again today, and to put yourself about a bit. At work you can get noticed and have some fantastic ideas that you need to put across to superiors. Don't worry if you think you are going over the top because that's what today is all about!

30 THURSDAY

Moon Age Day 10   Moon Sign Aries

You can soak up environmental influences like a sponge under present trends, and your sensitivity to others has rarely been better. Confidence remains potentially high and you have what it takes to overturn any obstacles that have been around for quite some time. Make the most of offers coming in from friends.

December
2006

1 FRIDAY
Moon Age Day 11   Moon Sign Aries

You should have continued scope to let yourself shine today, but in some practical ways you might be starting to run out of steam. Your best approach is to let others make some of the running, whilst you do your best to supervise. If there are some unusual circumstances surrounding family situations, you need to take these on board.

2 SATURDAY
Moon Age Day 12   Moon Sign Taurus

You may be trying to grasp a personal problem at the moment, but as with grabbing a nettle, you need to be firm. Treading on eggshells probably won't work and most people will be happy for you to say how you really feel. There are some gains to be made on the financial front, even if you aren't particularly trying to do so.

3 SUNDAY
Moon Age Day 13   Moon Sign Taurus

There is a slight tendency for you to scatter your energies today and you would be well advised to concentrate on one thing at once. If there are interesting people around this Sunday, you can gain a great deal from simply listening to what they have to say. A particular problem may solve itself.

4 MONDAY
Moon Age Day 14   Moon Sign Gemini

Wrong choices are possible today, and it is important to look at situations carefully and to take the advice that is on offer. You can't know everything, even though you sometimes think you do. Why not give yourself time to get to know people who come new into your life before you make any judgement?

5 TUESDAY *Moon Age Day 15 Moon Sign Gemini*

This would be a good time to sit back and take stock of progress you have been making recently. The lunar low doesn't encourage too much in the way of forward movement and you would be wise to let others make some of the running. With everything to play for later in the week, you can use this as a time of relaxation.

6 WEDNESDAY *Moon Age Day 16 Moon Sign Cancer*

There could be some slight tension underlying family relationships but such issues probably won't be around for long. Your best approach is to assess situations carefully and don't be too quick to jump to conclusions. A fine time for any sort of further education or at least for thinking about improving yourself in some way.

7 THURSDAY *Moon Age Day 17 Moon Sign Cancer*

You should have continued scope for advancement in your life generally and for letting your light shine, especially in a social sense. It might be only just occurring to you that Christmas is in view and that means a great many preparations. This week offers you the chance to make some of them.

8 FRIDAY *Moon Age Day 18 Moon Sign Cancer*

There might be a kind of see-sawing today between your personal desires and the things you know you should be doing for others. The demands and expectations that are presently coming in can seem a bit intimidating, but use your common sense and everything should turn out fine.

9 SATURDAY *Moon Age Day 19 Moon Sign Leo*

Mercury, now in your solar twelfth house, is characterised by faulty communication and a slight inability to get across the message you intend. Don't be too quick to make up your mind about anything early in the day. More favourable aspects take over later, leaving good scope for social possibilities by the evening.

10 SUNDAY   *Moon Age Day 20   Moon Sign Leo*

Emotional links you share with others are particularly strong at the present time, making this an ideal family time. Even if you want to get on well in the outside world, this might not be very easy today. Traditionally, Sunday is said to be a day of rest. Take note of the fact and have a steady sort of day.

11 MONDAY   *Moon Age Day 21   Moon Sign Virgo*

Professional matters definitely ought to be offering you significantly more than a 'business as usual' situation right now. It's time to take the bull by the horns and to let others know just how keen you are to get on. You have scope to turn someone you don't know too well into an important friend or ally.

12 TUESDAY   *Moon Age Day 22   Moon Sign Virgo*

There is both curiosity and a thirst for knowledge around now. Mercury has moved into your solar first house and offers better communication skills and a desire to get to the heart of almost any matter. With lots of energy and enthusiasm available to you, the remainder of this working week should suit you fine.

13 WEDNESDAY   *Moon Age Day 23   Moon Sign Libra*

You have what it takes to be quite lucky now in practical matters and are supported by the present position of Venus in your solar chart. Make the most of an upward turn in personal attachments, with romance figuring strongly in your life as a whole. Family relationships can also be made to look a good deal better.

14 THURSDAY   *Moon Age Day 24   Moon Sign Libra*

Trends suggest you have strong opinions to put forward, and though nobody is stopping you from doing so, you would be wise to temper this tendency with a little diplomacy. You can get your own way far better by approaching others gently than by trying to bulldoze people in a way they could tend to resent.

15 FRIDAY
Moon Age Day 25   Moon Sign Libra

The time is right to go full steam ahead with your dreams and schemes and not to let anything stand in the way. Positive thinking prevails and if you remain charming and determined, nobody is likely to oppose you. You don't need to argue with anyone at the moment because you are clearly in charge of most situations.

16 SATURDAY
Moon Age Day 26   Moon Sign Scorpio

For a very brief period the Moon enters your solar twelfth house and could hamper some of the forward motion you have been making for the last day or two. Don't worry about this. By early next week you can display more dynamism than ever, though for the moment you may have to settle for second-best.

17 SUNDAY
Moon Age Day 27   Moon Sign Scorpio

An enhancement to communication matters is on offer, even if today starts out a good deal slower than you might have wished. This would be a most opportune time to lay down some last-minute plans for Christmas. However, if you intend to go shopping now, you would be wise to watch your purse or wallet carefully.

18 MONDAY
Moon Age Day 28   Moon Sign Sagittarius

The lunar high offers a lift to your spirits and makes your efforts that much more likely to succeed. It's upward and onward for the next three days, with an enhanced ability to overcome restrictions and a determination on your part to have a good time. In a social sense it is possible that Christmas starts here for you.

19 TUESDAY
Moon Age Day 29Moon Sign Sagittarius

Certain choices you make today can be considered extremely fortunate, even if you haven't really looked at them or planned carefully. The fact is that if you get Lady Luck on your side, you can afford to take a few chances. Trends suggest that people you don't see very often may be making a return visit to your life.

20 WEDNESDAY   *Moon Age Day 0   Moon Sign Sagittarius*

It could well be towards business or practical matters that you now turn your attention. This is a good time to make new contacts that will be important for a long time to come. Socially speaking you have potential to be on top form and to show the world what the Archer is really like.

21 THURSDAY   *Moon Age Day 1   Moon Sign Capricorn*

The emphasis right now seems to be on material and personal indulgence, particularly if the Christmas parties have started already. You need to keep a clear head at present and there isn't much to be gained by overdoing things, especially in terms of food or drink. If you feel lethargic as a result, you will be annoyed with yourself.

22 FRIDAY   *Moon Age Day 2   Moon Sign Capricorn*

Financial matters could take a fortunate turn today and you may be better off than you expected. Don't be too quick to take offence at something a friend says, because chances are they mean no harm. There may be routines to be dealt with ahead of Christmas itself and some of these could prove irksome.

23 SATURDAY   *Moon Age Day 3   Moon Sign Aquarius*

Mars is now in your solar first house and this helps to bring out the 'battler' in you. It can never be forgotten that Sagittarius is a Fire sign and that when necessary you are willing to come out fighting. Right now you tend to be putting in all that effort on behalf of people you think might have been wronged.

24 SUNDAY   *Moon Age Day 4   Moon Sign Aquarius*

Something a friend says could enable you to broaden your horizons significantly today. In a more domestic sense you may well be wrapping up presents late into the night because Sagittarius is a natural 'last-minute Charlie'. In amongst everything else there ought to be time for simply enjoying yourself in the company of friends.

25 MONDAY
Moon Age Day 5   Moon Sign Pisces

With the planet of communication in your zodiac sign you can certainly make this a very chatty Christmas Day. You should have something kind to say to everyone and might decide that this is the time to bury a hatchet once and for all. Travel is possible later in the day and is well highlighted in your solar chart.

26 TUESDAY
Moon Age Day 6   Moon Sign Pisces

What trends encourage you to seek most of all right now is ease and comfort, so this may not be a particularly rip-roaring sort of Boxing Day. With a great desire to put others at their ease, you should be charming to know and can really lift the spirits of anyone who has been down in the dumps of late.

27 WEDNESDAY
Moon Age Day 7   Moon Sign Aries

In social gatherings you now have the ability to shine and can give of your best in most situations. Even if there are one or two awkward people about, probably family members, you can take such situations in your stride and bring warmth and humour to almost any encounter.

28 THURSDAY
Moon Age Day 8   Moon Sign Aries

A lucky financial phase is now on offer and this could prove to be a time during which you would rather spend than save. You may have your sights set on the post-Christmas sales and on something you have been coveting for quite some time. The gadget freaks amongst you are really in their element now!

29 FRIDAY
Moon Age Day 9   Moon Sign Taurus

Social and leisure pursuits are highlighted, and you probably won't be in the best frame of mind to deal with practicalities. If others are making heavy demands of you, the best way forward is to remind them gently that this is the holiday period and that you for one intend to enjoy it to the full.

30 SATURDAY
Moon Age Day 10   Moon Sign Taurus

The Moon is now in your solar sixth house and this could lead to a temporary absence of practical common sense. Before you commit yourself to anything major, it might be sensible to ask a friend for advice. Personalities could well enter your world around now and new friends are waiting in the wings.

31 SUNDAY
Moon Age Day 11   Moon Sign Taurus

This is a time when it might be best to suspend certain activities, in favour of simply soaking up the celebration that goes with the end of a year. Even if your level of energy is perhaps not quite what you would wish, you should still find the means to push the boat out as midnight approaches.

SAGITTARIUS:
2007 DIARY PAGES

SAGITTARIUS: 2007 IN BRIEF

The advice to Sagittarius this year is to start as you mean to go on. The sooner you are in gear at the start of January, the greater is the chance that you will start to make significant advances. It might take a few days to get things working the way you want, and memories of the Christmas break will stay with you for the first part of January, but in the main you will soon be committed to the new year. January and February both bring new opportunities and offer better incentives at work. Personal relationships are strong at this time.

The early spring months of March and April should find you generally in the pink. You know what you want from life and in most situations have a very good idea how to get it. Your usual optimistic nature is on display and you should be in a very good position to move forward at work. Family members might be giving you the odd problem but these should soon be sorted out, leaving you with enough time to follow your own incentives and dreams.

By the time May arrives you will probably be wrestling with issues that have been important to you for some time, but situations you haven't been able to address before. Your attitude will be very positive and there are possible financial gains, both through good luck and also because of your tenacity. June will be similar but carries a slightly nostalgic aspect that makes you somewhat more reflective. This is likely to disappear during July because you become far more committed to the future and to projects you know can make you better off. Long-term thinking is important during both July and August, and though you often throw caution to the wind, this is a period where more care is necessary and a time during which you have to concentrate.

With the arrival of the autumn, September and October are likely to be perhaps a little quieter than earlier months, but none the less useful for that. This is a time to think deeply and to build on plans you have already laid. Romance may be stronger around now than at any other time this year, and some Archers will be making a totally new start in terms of loving relationships.

November and December are likely to be months of significant activity, and will mark a time during which you are generally cheerful, committed to life fully and well able to use your intuition, which is extremely strong at this time. Advantages come through family relationships, possible new romantic attachments and as a result of a hobby that could turn out to be much more. Christmas should be busy and exciting, with you taking centre stage as usual.

1 MONDAY
Moon Age Day 13   Moon Sign Gemini

This may not turn out to be the most dynamic of starts to a new year. The Moon occupies your opposite zodiac sign of Gemini, a time of month known as the lunar low. A little extra concentration would be useful and you may not achieve the mental high that Sagittarius is usually seeking.

2 TUESDAY
Moon Age Day 14   Moon Sign Gemini

If things are still not quite the way you would wish them to be, one option is to rely more on the good offices of others. There are individuals around from whom you can get assistance, and by the end of today you should be back on course. Romance is possible by the evening.

3 WEDNESDAY
Moon Age Day 15   Moon Sign Cancer

There are strong domestic rewards available now for Archers who spend extra time at home. At this time of year you probably won't want to be charging about from pillar to post, although it has to be remembered that a long Christmas break may have made you somewhat restless. Why not try to ring the changes when you can?

4 THURSDAY
Moon Age Day 16   Moon Sign Cancer

Trends encourage you to look towards recreation today, and it shouldn't be hard to mix business with pleasure. Getting others to do your bidding should not be too hard, and you can persuade some of them to pay you back for favours you have shown them in the past.

5 FRIDAY
Moon Age Day 17   Moon Sign Leo

Your social life is now apt to bring significant surprises, and could prompt you to do things you hadn't really planned, possibly as a result of the encouragement of friends. With the weekend in view you have scope to organise things so that you can have a good time, particularly if you are not inclined towards work right now.

6 SATURDAY
Moon Age Day 18   Moon Sign Leo

There could be a little more in the way of inner reflection possible today, but not for very long. This would be an ideal time to catch up with the January sales, and you can almost certainly get yourself in the right frame of mind to be spending money. Make the most of chances to contact people who are re-entering your life now.

7 SUNDAY
Moon Age Day 19   Moon Sign Virgo

The present position of the Sun heralds a slightly more restless trend and you may be quite happy to go with the flow in a social sense, though not if that means standing still for too long. If routines bore you, try to do something different whenever possible today.

8 MONDAY
Moon Age Day 20   Moon Sign Virgo

If you emphasise your personality today you will get on far better. What you don't want is to be passed by at a time when you need to shine in order to get on in your own estimation. It really is what you feel about yourself that matters the most at the moment, because to the Archer, confidence is everything.

9 TUESDAY
Moon Age Day 21   Moon Sign Virgo

You are now entering a period during which you have what it takes to stand out in a crowd. Don't be too quick to criticise others, particularly at work, otherwise you may only serve to emphasise your own shortcomings. There are some distinct advantages to be gained by being in the right place at the most opportune time.

10 WEDNESDAY *Moon Age Day 22   Moon Sign Libra*

Your originality is heightened and you have what it takes to turn heads. This means you can get on especially well at work and in any situation that offers you scope to get into the public eye. Now is the time to show your humour and to make a joke out of even slightly embarrassing situations.

11 THURSDAY *Moon Age Day 23   Moon Sign Libra*

It looks as though you might need to be just a little more careful with money at present, particularly if there are amounts to spend that you did not expect. You can make more money in the longer-term, but for the moment your interests are best served if you keep your purse or wallet closed to new purchases.

12 FRIDAY *Moon Age Day 24   Moon Sign Scorpio*

What a good day this can be with regard to romance. It's worth keeping your options open, especially if you are not presently involved in a personal relationship, and being willing to go with the flow in every social sense. Life should look after you if you just show how much confidence you have in yourself.

13 SATURDAY *Moon Age Day 25   Moon Sign Scorpio*

It might be somewhat difficult to make decisions today, particularly if there is more than one option and they all look particularly good. If the attitude of a friend or a family member is somewhat difficult to understand, you need to be just a little careful not to give unintentional offence.

14 SUNDAY *Moon Age Day 26   Moon Sign Scorpio*

You have scope to put a great driving force behind your actions now, and to make the most favourable of impressions on other people. You can't expect to achieve everything you would wish, but there are good options for making alterations in and around your home.

15 MONDAY   *Moon Age Day 27   Moon Sign Sagittarius*

It shouldn't be hard to attract the good things in life this week, so why not start as you mean to go on? The Moon has entered your zodiac sign, bringing that time of the month known as the lunar high. This means that you have better opportunities than usual and can push yourself harder than has been the case recently.

16 TUESDAY   *Moon Age Day 28   Moon Sign Sagittarius*

You can still make sure things look good in a general sense, even if you lack patience when it comes to sorting out the details of life. Attitude is everything and you certainly have plenty today. Acting on impulse is what you were born to do, and trends assist you to get away with just about anything right now.

17 WEDNESDAY   *Moon Age Day 29   Moon Sign Capricorn*

Today works best if you remain assertive and let the world know exactly what you want from it. Rather than being vague, you would be wise to focus on those matters that you know to be the most important in a practical and a financial sense. Personal attachments may not receive too much attention now.

18 THURSDAY   *Moon Age Day 0   Moon Sign Capricorn*

Today is better when it comes to addressing relationships, and you should have more time and patience to do those things that make others happy. You still might not be too happy when faced with what you see as being pointless rules and regulations. Be prepared to keep up your efforts for personal advancement at work.

19 FRIDAY   *Moon Age Day 1   Moon Sign Aquarius*

The end of the working week for many of you brings a day during which some frustrations are possible. It might well be difficult to get others round to your way of thinking. This can be particularly hard when you know in your own mind that what you believe is absolutely true.

20 SATURDAY   *Moon Age Day 2   Moon Sign Aquarius*

Your best approach is to show a great deal of self-discipline and avoid getting bogged down with pointless details, which always irritate you. Even though the weekend has arrived you can get more done in a practical sense than you expected, and can also make a favourable social impression when it matters the most.

21 SUNDAY   *Moon Age Day 3   Moon Sign Aquarius*

There is great optimism about now and a chance for you to get things going your way. Although you may be slightly hampered in your efforts to get ahead financially, that isn't really what today is all about. Rather, you can use this time to make headway in all attachments, both personal ones and simple friendship.

22 MONDAY   *Moon Age Day 4   Moon Sign Pisces*

There are possible gains today, especially those of a personal nature. At the same time you need to be careful not to offer any unintentional offence. You can't expect everyone to be on your side, and it's worth trying to be reasonable when it comes to dealing with anyone who has a very different point of view.

23 TUESDAY   *Moon Age Day 5   Moon Sign Pisces*

This has potential to be a hectic period and a time during which you might have to work hard in order to keep up with all that is expected of you. Don't be surprised if someone you don't see too often returns to your life and brings with them a breath of fresh air. As usual you should be keen to persuade everyone about your strong points.

24 WEDNESDAY   *Moon Age Day 6   Moon Sign Aries*

Though your domestic life is well highlighted at this time you may have to work very hard in order to persuade a disbelieving few that you know what you are talking about. For once you might be slightly tongue-tied, and this is so unusual for Sagittarius that it could be seen as unique!

25 THURSDAY
Moon Age Day 7   Moon Sign Aries

Although you can enjoy today, you could find that there are changes in the offing at work that you don't care for the look of. Before you raise direct objections it would be sensible to think things through very carefully. By the end of the day you can afford to have your mind set on socialising.

26 FRIDAY
Moon Age Day 8   Moon Sign Taurus

The end of the week arrives at last, offering you scope to let your hair down. With plenty of cheek and that silver-tongue working again on your behalf, you shouldn't have any trouble at all making friends. The attitude of someone close to you may be slightly difficult to understand.

27 SATURDAY
Moon Age Day 9   Moon Sign Taurus

The focus is on thinking about personal goals and objectives at the moment, and you may decide to let the responsibilities of your life take a holiday. This would be a good day for a shopping spree or for thinking about some very early but quite necessary spring-cleaning.

28 SUNDAY
Moon Age Day 10   Moon Sign Gemini

Now is the time to pay more attention to the feelings of others, particularly at home. The fact is that you could well be upsetting someone without remotely intending to do so. There are occasions when the Archer speaks without thinking, and that may be the problem that lies at the back of any difficulties that arise now.

29 MONDAY
Moon Age Day 11   Moon Sign Gemini

You can make sure you are well appreciated by most of the people you come across at the moment, which is just as well because you may decide to call upon their assistance whilst the lunar low is around. Trends are not helping you to work at your best, and you might benefit from a few hours to yourself at some stage today.

30 TUESDAY   *Moon Age Day 12   Moon Sign Cancer*

Your powers of attraction are strong, making this an ideal period from a romantic point of view. Even if not everyone falls prey to your charms, you should be able to persuade someone that you are fantastic. Let us hope for your sake that this is the person who is 'supposed' to be the most important individual in your life!

31 WEDNESDAY   *Moon Age Day 13   Moon Sign Cancer*

Look for a little nostalgia at the moment by all means, but don't live in the past. The Archer is generally committed to the future rather than the past and you can get a little down in the dumps if you dwell on things too much. You can use the positive attitude of friends to enhance your own happiness.

February

2007

1 THURSDAY
Moon Age Day 14   Moon Sign Leo

If domestic situations are somewhat strained, you may be trying your best to put right situations that are not going quite as you would wish. There could be slight problems with younger family members, but on a professional footing you have what it takes to be working hard and making progress.

2 FRIDAY
Moon Age Day 15   Moon Sign Leo

This is definitely a good time during which to take a centre-stage position. Trends assist you to be snappy, good to know and very, very exciting to have around. If there are people who don't quite realise what you are worth, leave them along and concentrate on those who have no difficulty seeing your magic.

3 SATURDAY
Moon Age Day 16   Moon Sign Leo

Even if you are very busy this weekend, it's worth leaving hours free during which you can have a good time. This doesn't mean having to achieve something concrete, and you can be just as happy in the company of freewheeling types who have no agenda. Just let life happen and enjoy the ride!

4 SUNDAY
Moon Age Day 17   Moon Sign Virgo

A smooth period of achieving your objectives and enjoying the company of family members seems to be what you can accomplish on this Sunday. It's possible you are not really getting anywhere fast, but the planetary line-up at the moment doesn't really demand that you should. Romance especially looks good.

5 MONDAY
Moon Age Day 18   Moon Sign Virgo

Trends encourage you to be fairly ambitious today and to get on quickly with anything that is on your mind. The only problem is that your friends and colleagues may not feel quite the same way. However, even if you have to go it alone you have the ability to make real progress.

6 TUESDAY
Moon Age Day 19   Moon Sign Virgo

Your self-confidence is still highlighted, and there may well be some pleasant surprises on offer around now. You might have difficulty understanding the motivations of those who are especially close to you, and more attention could be needed with regard to family matters.

7 WEDNESDAY
Moon Age Day 20   Moon Sign Libra

Even if you remain generally happy with your lot, you may have to modify your ideas at short-notice for maximum gain. This shouldn't be at all hard for the Archer, and you prove yourself to be as adaptable as ever. An ideal day to contact valued friends, especially those who are far from home at present.

8 THURSDAY
Moon Age Day 21   Moon Sign Libra

Beneficial material trends seem to be around, but you can't really afford to gamble too much because you could find yourself coming unstuck. Routines seem fairly comfortable, and these perpetuate throughout most of today and well into tomorrow. Romance is to the fore now and closer to the weekend.

9 FRIDAY
Moon Age Day 22   Moon Sign Scorpio

A slightly quieter spell overtakes you as the Moon passes through your solar twelfth house. The focus is on being more contemplative and looking at situations more carefully, giving time to decisions and getting things generally right. Don't be too quick to form a judgement regarding a particular family issue.

10 SATURDAY   *Moon Age Day 23   Moon Sign Scorpio*

Even though the weekend has arrived you will probably find things to do and might be rather more preoccupied than is presently good for you. With the afternoon you can afford to take some time out to do whatever takes your fancy, most likely in the company of the person who is most important to you.

11 SUNDAY   *Moon Age Day 24   Moon Sign Scorpio*

By tomorrow you can get right on the ball and be pushing forward positively, but today offers you a chance to remain slightly dreamy and not over-anxious to do anything of consequence. The time of year won't inspire you too much, but you should still feel better if you get out of the house into the fresh air.

12 MONDAY   *Moon Age Day 25   Moon Sign Sagittarius*

The Moon returns to your zodiac sign, brining the lunar high for February. Now you can get yourself motivated, and can use this interlude to tackle a mountain of work. You get things done whilst others are still thinking about it, and you should have little trouble making up your mind about anything.

13 TUESDAY   *Moon Age Day 26   Moon Sign Sagittarius*

The more ambitious you are with your dreams and schemes, the better you can make things turn out for you in the real world. Your nature is electrifying and you shouldn't have any trouble making the most favourable of impressions in any company. Having a good sense of proportion probably won't help you today.

14 WEDNESDAY ☿ *Moon Age Day 27   Moon Sign Capricorn*

You realise how important first impressions can be, and may now decide to spend a good deal of your time bringing people round to your specific point of view. This is achieved with a combination of flattery and gentle bullying. You might see this as being essential, not only for your sake but for theirs too.

15 THURSDAY ☿ *Moon Age Day 28   Moon Sign Capricorn*

Don't be afraid to focus on political matters, nor to show your strong social conscience. Supporting people who are going through a hard time comes as second nature to you at the moment and you can be especially kind to those whose thought processes don't work as quickly as yours.

16 FRIDAY ☿ *Moon Age Day 0   Moon Sign Aquarius*

You can probably get further with your career ambitions now than at any other time during February. Your strength lies in deciding what you want and having a very good idea how you are going to go about getting it. Don't expect to get the whole world on your side, though you should be able to convince the people who matter the most.

17 SATURDAY ☿ *Moon Age Day 1   Moon Sign Aquarius*

The hectic pace that has been possible for the last few days continues now, and you remain capable of making a good impression, even on those occasions when it doesn't really matter at all. With everything to play for in terms of general and sporting activities, you needn't settle for second-best.

18 SUNDAY ☿ *Moon Age Day 2   Moon Sign Pisces*

Progress remains possible, though this being a Sunday you might not expect to be getting too much done. In any case it could be good to spend some time with your partner or family members, and too much go-getting could so easily get in the way of simple enjoyment.

19 MONDAY ☿ *Moon Age Day 3   Moon Sign Pisces*

There are signs that some of your present aims and objectives might be slightly unrealistic, and it might be sensible to look at a few of them again, this time paying more attention. Outside of practicalities you have scope to adopt new interests and some of these are likely to have a distinctly intellectual bias.

20 TUESDAY ☿ *Moon Age Day 4   Moon Sign Aries*

For those Sagittarians who have been slightly off colour during the last couple of days, present trends are now likely to be looking better. Don't be too worried if loved ones seem a touch out of sorts, but pay them the attention they deserve and be there for them if they want to talk.

21 WEDNESDAY ☿ *Moon Age Day 5   Moon Sign Aries*

If getting to the root of a personal issue is your intention today, you could well be quieter and more contemplative around now. It could be that you are worrying about nothing in particular, but that will not prevent you from niggling about things all the same.

22 THURSDAY ☿ *Moon Age Day 6   Moon Sign Taurus*

It is towards friendship and social activities that you are encouraged to turn at the moment, and you can now find romance to be especially rewarding. The Archer can now afford to take time out to look closely at specific issues, and this helps you to avoid making mistakes, and to pursue small successes.

23 FRIDAY ☿ *Moon Age Day 7   Moon Sign Taurus*

You could well feel a strong need now to do things entirely your own way, even if you have to upset one or two people as a result. You would be wise to avoid getting bogged down with pointless routines, particularly if these bore you. In any case you can benefit from a dose of genuine action ahead of the lunar low.

24 SATURDAY ☿ *Moon Age Day 8   Moon Sign Gemini*

A period of withdrawal is possible for some Archers across this weekend. With the lunar low around you may not be pushing over any buses, and might be quite happy to spend time in the bosom of your family. An ideal period to sit back and watch life go by, whilst you enjoy watching others occasionally make a mess of things.

25 SUNDAY ☿ *Moon Age Day 9   Moon Sign Gemini*

With the lunar low around you may not be exactly dynamic, but you needn't lose that impish sense of humour at all. It's worth keeping a sense of proportion regarding family matters and getting out of doors if you can. This is not a time during which you should be taking yourself or anyone else too seriously.

26 MONDAY ☿ *Moon Age Day 10   Moon Sign Gemini*

For the third day in a row the Moon occupies the sign of Gemini, which doesn't assist you to get ahead too much, at least not early in the day. By lunchtime you have what it takes to be more outgoing and to mix with those you find refreshing to be around.

27 TUESDAY ☿ *Moon Age Day 11   Moon Sign Cancer*

There are possible pleasant activities to undertake now, most likely in the company of those you count as good friends. At the same time you can be extremely communicative, and can use this trait as an excuse to make contact with others. Important news is available from family members.

28 WEDNESDAY ☿ *Moon Age Day 12   Moon Sign Cancer*

Your dealings with others show you to be very diplomatic and entirely capable of using a strengthening intuition. Practical common sense is fine, but when you are overtaken by a very definite feeling about anything it is important to listen carefully. Why not spend some time with your partner if at all possible today?

 **2007**

1 THURSDAY ☿ *Moon Age Day 13   Moon Sign Leo*

The first day of a new month offers an opportunity to get ahead and possibly to be more outspoken than has been the case for a number of days. This is due to the position of Mars in your solar chart. The only slight fly in the ointment is that you could be rather too harsh in your judgements and inclined to be critical.

2 FRIDAY ☿ *Moon Age Day 14   Moon Sign Leo*

The Archer can be just a little selfish at the moment, and it would be sensible to analyse your motivations in anything before proceeding. What you don't need right now is to make an enemy, especially as it isn't necessary to do so. Today works best if you can balance your dynamic attitude with a tendency towards diplomacy.

3 SATURDAY ☿ *Moon Age Day 15   Moon Sign Virgo*

There appear to be good trends developing in personal attachments, and you could be slightly better to know today. You may decide to get to grips with things that need doing at home, especially out in the garden. A dose of fresh air should help to blow away the cobwebs and enable you to feel alert and happy.

4 SUNDAY ☿ *Moon Age Day 16   Moon Sign Virgo*

You can ensure that anyone you meet around now will have a big part to play in your longer-term future. All the planetary trends show that this is a good time to make new friends and you can have a strong influence on the way others think. When approaching anything new, attitude is all-important.

5 MONDAY ☿ *Moon Age Day 17   Moon Sign Virgo*

You can make this a rather good day from a personal point of view, with plenty to keep you occupied and some new social input available. Relationships could work especially well for you, and you have scope to have plenty of interaction with people who are in a position to offer you some assistance.

6 TUESDAY ☿ *Moon Age Day 18   Moon Sign Libra*

Trends indicate that you have a greater than average need to express yourself at present, which is surprising bearing in mind that the Archer rarely stops talking in any case. It isn't so much what you are saying today that matters but the sort of people with whom you are in contact. Once again, seeking some timely help can work wonders.

7 WEDNESDAY ☿ *Moon Age Day 19   Moon Sign Libra*

There are gains to be made by showing interest in the world at large and by getting yourself involved in new activities of one sort or another. Your capacity to mix business with pleasure has hardly ever been better, and you can use this skill to sort out some sort of mess created by a loved one.

8 THURSDAY ☿ *Moon Age Day 20   Moon Sign Scorpio*

Chances are that you will still be putting others first, something that helps you to get yourself noticed in the right circles. Don't think just because others are quiet that they are not paying attention. Almost every move you make may be being monitored by one person or another, so it's worth being on your best behaviour.

9 FRIDAY *Moon Age Day 21   Moon Sign Scorpio*

If you get the chance to break the bounds of the normal and to do something completely different today, you should grab the opportunity with both hands. Getting down to some hard work might not be too appealing but you will be glad you applied yourself when the benefits start to come in.

10 SATURDAY *Moon Age Day 22   Moon Sign Scorpio*

Even if Saturday doesn't turn out to be very exciting, you may not care too much. The Moon is in your solar twelfth house and that encourages you to be more contemplative than usual and quite willing to stand and watch for a while. Don't be surprised if relatives give you good reason to be proud of them.

11 SUNDAY *Moon Age Day 23   Moon Sign Sagittarius*

The lunar high offers new incentives, and even though this is a Sunday you can afford to try something different, especially in a social sense. You can also use this interlude to get yourself ready for what could be a busy week that lies ahead, and a little prior planning now should pay dividends later.

12 MONDAY *Moon Age Day 24   Moon Sign Sagittarius*

Your strength lies in applying yourself fully from the moment you rise this morning and taking advantage of the very real possibilities that this day contains. You may be acting almost entirely on impulse, but you are so insightful that you can make all manner of gains without really trying. Most important of all, your popularity is potentially high.

13 TUESDAY *Moon Age Day 25   Moon Sign Capricorn*

For probably the first time this month you are in a position to look at personal relationships extremely closely. If you honestly feel that you haven't been doing enough to prove to your partner just how important they are to you, now is the time to turn on the charm and show how you really feel.

14 WEDNESDAY *Moon Age Day 26   Moon Sign Capricorn*

If things are not going fast enough for you right now, you do have what it takes to speed life up. This takes extra effort and it is true that there may be a slightly lazy streak about you at present. The ideal situation would be to make gains as a result of the actions of others, whilst you watch on and applaud.

15 THURSDAY   *Moon Age Day 27*   *Moon Sign Capricorn*

Both internal and external pressures are evident under present trends, though you needn't let these slow you down appreciably. However, it might be quite annoying to discover that no matter how hard you work someone else seems to be doing everything they can to negate your effort.

16 FRIDAY   *Moon Age Day 28*   *Moon Sign Aquarius*

You can't expect to be on the ball through every moment of the day on this March Friday, but if you restrict yourself to one activity at once, you stand the best chance of working things out reasonably well. You may not be exactly firing on all cylinders but if you bluff your way through the day that shouldn't matter either.

17 SATURDAY   *Moon Age Day 29*   *Moon Sign Aquarius*

If there is a slight problem today it probably comes from the fact that you want everything to turn out the way you would wish and that might not be possible. It might be better if you restrict your interference a little, because it's no use trying to do everyone's job as well as your own.

18 SUNDAY   *Moon Age Day 0*   *Moon Sign Pisces*

If there are any decisions to be made, you could hardly choose a better day than this. Your reasoning is sound and you can find sufficient time to think about things. Having to alter your social diary quite a bit might be something of a bore, but what you can come up with for today should be interesting enough, even if it's unexpected.

19 MONDAY   *Moon Age Day 1*   *Moon Sign Pisces*

Trends assist you to look carefully at matters that have a bearing on your home life and the area in which you live. You might even decide to become involved in some sort of pressure group, or to fight the corner of individuals who cannot stand up for themselves as much as you can.

20 TUESDAY
Moon Age Day 2   Moon Sign Aries

You need to be much more selective, especially about who you call a close friend. Not everyone is worthy of the name, though the people you have known for a long time should come good under all circumstances. Now is the time to keep your eyes open, because deception is possible under present planetary trends.

21 WEDNESDAY
Moon Age Day 3   Moon Sign Aries

If you have been putting a great deal of effort into work projects, it's possible that you could be able to attract reward or recognition now. It isn't hard for you to concentrate on several different things at the same time, and your lightning thought processes could even baffle some people.

22 THURSDAY
Moon Age Day 4   Moon Sign Taurus

A day to take time out to look more carefully at your personal life. The trouble is that you get so busy you don't always pay as much attention as you should to the person with whom you share your life. You can afford to make a special fuss of them today, and even if there is no anniversary to celebrate you could invent one!

23 FRIDAY
Moon Age Day 5   Moon Sign Taurus

There is a certain restlessness about Sagittarius right now. This is partly to do with the advancing year and the better weather, but is also inspired by planetary movements in your solar chart. You need to make a break with the mundane in some way, and any sort of trip would probably do you no end of good now.

24 SATURDAY
Moon Age Day 6   Moon Sign Gemini

You may not get everything you want today, and the more so because the Moon has now moved into your opposite zodiac sign. The lunar low needn't cause you too many problems this time around but you may decide to restrict your actions in some way or else make changes to plans at the last minute.

25 SUNDAY   *Moon Age Day 7   Moon Sign Gemini*

It's worth settling for something quiet and relaxing if that proves to be at all possible today. Don't get bogged down with boring jobs and if they simply have to be done, get them out of the way early in the day. Why not make contact with people you don't see very often, or even arrange an impromtu meeting?

26 MONDAY   *Moon Age Day 8   Moon Sign Cancer*

The lunar low is now well out of the way, leaving you in a fairly positive position to face a new week. Be prepared to catch up with communications today and make sure that you keep others informed of what you are planning to do. The only real problem will come if you fail to get your intentions across to the world.

27 TUESDAY   *Moon Age Day 9   Moon Sign Cancer*

There should be hardly anything today that will faze you and you can take great delight in doing things for the first time. Not everyone is equally confident and you may have to offer a good deal of support from time to time. This will be especially true in the case of timorous colleagues or younger family members.

28 WEDNESDAY   *Moon Age Day 10   Moon Sign Leo*

Even if you want to do all you can to help people today, it may not always be possible. You need to look at your own life too and to do all you can to get things straight for a big push that is just around the corner. Spending time with loved ones in the evening might be both appealing and rewarding.

29 THURSDAY   *Moon Age Day 11   Moon Sign Leo*

You need to be on the ball when it comes to making decisions today, and shouldn't be in the least upset if people criticise you. You can be very accommodating at the moment and more than willing to look at a particular matter again, in a new and very different light. The time is right to help younger family members.

30 FRIDAY
Moon Age Day 12   Moon Sign Leo

There is a great deal of optimism available at the present time, and an opportunity to commit yourself to new and interesting strategies. The Archer is coming into its own in all sorts of ways and there are exciting new potentials around every corner. Giving help to a friend can work wonders under present influences.

31 SATURDAY
Moon Age Day 13   Moon Sign Virgo

Your great generosity of spirit is   highlighted, and you could be doing all you can to help those who are less well off than you are. If you have any trip planned for the moment, so much the better because you respond well to a change of scene and to new and interesting possibilities that are on offer.

2007

1 SUNDAY
Moon Age Day 14   Moon Sign Virgo

Once again if you get the chance to travel you should grab the opportunity with both hands. There are some interesting diversions available, and new people to meet. What probably pleases you the most at present is being able to help out those who have got themselves into something of a muddle.

2 MONDAY
Moon Age Day 15   Moon Sign Libra

You can help yourself greatly now by doing something that isn't strictly necessary but which you know will make the future easier for all concerned. Romance is well accented throughout the whole of this week, and you have what it takes to turn heads in a social as well as a personal sense.

3 TUESDAY
Moon Age Day 16   Moon Sign Libra

The time is right to get away from unhealthy or unproductive situations. If you are on a kick towards making yourself fitter, you need to concentrate, but beware of going at things like a bull at a gate. One major change to your life is better than half a dozen half-hearted ones. Sagittarian commitment is legendary, but it can wear you out.

4 WEDNESDAY
Moon Age Day 17   Moon Sign Libra

Family matters tend to be very rewarding now, and you may decide to spend as much time as you can with loved ones. Keeping confidences is vital, because people are relying on you and won't take kindly to you spreading their business far and wide. Most important of all you need to be careful in whom you confide.

5 THURSDAY   *Moon Age Day 18   Moon Sign Scorpio*

Even if you seem to have plenty of energy today, you may actually get very little done. For this you can thank a twelfth-house Moon, and in all honesty it might be best to curtail some of your efforts for a day or two. Progress is once again possible in romance.

6 FRIDAY   *Moon Age Day 19   Moon Sign Scorpio*

Your best approach is to keep your purse or wallet firmly closed today unless you are certain that a bargain is in the offing. There's a chance you could be duped at the moment and there is nothing you can do about the situation except to show extreme caution. Not a very good day to sign documents unless you have read the small print.

7 SATURDAY   *Moon Age Day 20   Moon Sign Sagittarius*

The Moon moves back into your zodiac sign and makes for one of the most potentially exciting weekends so far this year. All it takes is a little effort from you and you can make sure things turn out fine. You know how to have a good time and are in a positon to take others along with you.

8 SUNDAY   *Moon Age Day 21   Moon Sign Sagittarius*

A day to drop all pretence and leave alone those tasks that are best undertaken when you are in a less excitable frame of mind. Be prepared to find someone who is as keen to get on as you are and break the bounds of the usual. You can now use your charm to achieve significant popularity in all groups.

9 MONDAY   *Moon Age Day 22   Moon Sign Sagittarius*

You might want to turn on the charm at the beginning of this week because there is no doubt it can get you a long way. Not everyone is susceptible of course, but people who insist on being miserable needn't have much of a part to play in your life just at the moment. You probably prefer those who are cheerful and happy.

10 TUESDAY   *Moon Age Day 23   Moon Sign Capricorn*

It is the practical aspects of life that are highlighted today. You want to get things done and the best way you know is to get stuck in. Conforming to expectations may not always be easy, particularly if you want to do everything your own way. The Archer can be a bit unreasonable now.

11 WEDNESDAY   *Moon Age Day 24   Moon Sign Capricorn*

This may not be your luckiest day, and you could well have to work extra hard to get where you want to be. Once again you might have to control your irrepressible desire to move ahead in the face of some obstacles. You should at least be able to get romance working the way you would wish.

12 THURSDAY   *Moon Age Day 25   Moon Sign Aquarius*

There are times today when you can prove to be positively inspirational but at the same time there may be obstacles being placed in your path. It's worth starting early in the day with practical jobs and that way you can have a few hours later to please yourself. If possible find time for a breath of fresh air.

13 FRIDAY   *Moon Age Day 26   Moon Sign Aquarius*

There could be some frustrations with personal objectives, but in the main you can make sure things are looking better. Rather than going for a confrontational approach today, it pays to remain as diplomatic as possible. Romantic overtures are on offer for the young or young-at-heart Sagittarian now.

14 SATURDAY   *Moon Age Day 27   Moon Sign Pisces*

Trends encourage you to do everything you can to maximise your potential at the moment, and the weekend is no block to your forward progress in life. You should be feeling better about yourself and more able to move forward on a number of fronts. Finances might look stronger, even if this is something of an illusion.

15 SUNDAY   *Moon Age Day 28   Moon Sign Pisces*

Some of you will have one eye firmly on the past today. Why this should be the case might seem like something of a puzzle. Even if you are analysing things that have happened before and taking some lessons from past events, you would be wise to keep at least one eye on the present and the future.

16 MONDAY   *Moon Age Day 29   Moon Sign Aries*

This has potential to be one of the most assertive days of the month as far as you are concerned. It could be difficult getting others motivated and that is one of your tests for today. If colleagues seem unwilling to commit themselves, some gentle shoving may well be necessary.

17 TUESDAY   *Moon Age Day 0   Moon Sign Aries*

You should be able to express yourself well at the moment – not that this is generally an issue for the Archer. If you are happy and generally content with your lot, you can make sure you are entertaining to have around and can always think up new schemes to keep people smiling. The Archer can be a practical joker at present.

18 WEDNESDAY   *Moon Age Day 1   Moon Sign Taurus*

It is the intimate side of your life that is highlighted now. If you want to find some way to show your partner or sweetheart just how important they are to you, your best response is to turn your originality up to full. Not everyone responds to your charm, but you can't please everyone.

19 THURSDAY   *Moon Age Day 2   Moon Sign Taurus*

It's worth staying busy and productive today, because there are a couple of days ahead during which you may be far less motivated. Why not cast your mind forward to journeys you want to make and do some of the planning for them right now? This may involve getting in touch with someone at a distance.

20 FRIDAY
Moon Age Day 3   Moon Sign Gemini

You have what it takes to remain generally popular with others, but might not feel particularly inspired. The reason is the lunar low, and you may decide there isn't really much point in starting anything too demanding for the next couple of days. Many Archers will be coasting along and relying on efforts they made some time ago.

21 SATURDAY
Moon Age Day 4   Moon Sign Gemini

Another day dawns during which your best approach is to rely on the good offices and common sense of those around you. You stand on the riverbank of life and tend to watch the water flowing past. This isn't an especially comfortable procedure for Sagittarius, but is necessary now and again.

22 SUNDAY
Moon Age Day 5   Moon Sign Cancer

With the lunar low now out of the way and other planetary influences predominating, now is the time to let your sense of wonder and your enquiring mind take over. Don't settle for the ordinary today but rather stretch yourself to look at matters that are beyond your usual sphere of experience.

23 MONDAY
Moon Age Day 6   Moon Sign Cancer

Trends encourage a very practical turn of mind today and a desire to get things done, especially at work. You have the ability to instigate plenty of co-operation, and it looks as though you should get on very well when in group situations. Don't be surprised if others insist that you take the lead.

24 TUESDAY
Moon Age Day 7   Moon Sign Leo

Although some caution is indicated today, this needn't prevent you from taking chances. Sagittarius sometimes rushes in where angels fear to tread, but you usually get away with it. Your powers of communication are well starred, and you have the look of someone who could sell fridges to Eskimos at the moment.

25 WEDNESDAY   *Moon Age Day 8   Moon Sign Leo*

The Moon is now in Leo, from where it casts a favourable light on your own zodiac sign of Sagittarius. This highlights your cheefulness and your willingness to go with the flow in any work or social situation. Your desire for personal progress remains strong, as does your tendency to demand much of yourself.

26 THURSDAY   *Moon Age Day 9   Moon Sign Leo*

There isn't much doubt about your optimism at present, but you might have to curb it now and again in favour of practical and sound judgements. Of course you want to show everyone how capable you are, but unless you exercise just a little care and caution you could come unstuck in a particularly embarrassing way.

27 FRIDAY   *Moon Age Day 10   Moon Sign Virgo*

You have what it takes to make a favourable impression and should be feeling very joyful about personal attachments. If there is some sort of anniversary in the offing you need to do all you can to make it very special. Conforming to the expectations of superiors or colleagues might not be too easy.

28 SATURDAY   *Moon Age Day 11   Moon Sign Virgo*

It's true that there may be challenges about, but these only add to your desire to get ahead in a general sense. Change and diversity are favoured around now, and its' worth ringing the changes as far as your social life is concerned. A day to get in touch with family members and maybe arrange a reunion of some sort.

29 SUNDAY   *Moon Age Day 12   Moon Sign Libra*

Although you can give financial matters some sort of boost at the moment, you need to be careful about how much you spread cash around. The things that are most important to you on this spring Sunday come completely free of charge, which is why you don't have to spend much to enjoy the day.

30 MONDAY
Moon Age Day 13   Moon Sign Libra

Doing more than one job at once is so much a part of your nature that it should present you with little or no challenge right now. Be prepared to start the week as you mean to go on and to show a very positive face towards work. When your commitments are out of the way, there is scope for you to find new methods for having fun.

2007

1 TUESDAY
Moon Age Day 14   Moon Sign Libra

Your curiosity seems to be leading you at the start of May, and you can also make the most of that great joy of realising that the year is growing older and that the warm weather is now on the way. This encourages you to spread your wings, and even if you can't go anywhere today, you can at least dream and plan.

2 WEDNESDAY
Moon Age Day 15   Moon Sign Scorpio

A slower sort of day is indicated, but this doesn't mean you can't make any impression on life. It is simply that you should be steadier in your approach and slightly more thoughtful than might sometimes be the case. This could leave you with time to spend on family members, some of whom need your support.

3 THURSDAY
Moon Age Day 16   Moon Sign Scorpio

Domestic situations are indicated as being the most important ones for today. Although you may be quite busy at work your mind might be at home, and you have scope to do all you can to support family members and especially younger ones. Trends assist you to remain cheerful and, in the main, optimistic.

4 FRIDAY
Moon Age Day 17   Moon Sign Sagittarius

The lunar high offers you an ideal chance to be as charming as can be and very committed to projects that are presently on your mind. At the same time you can get Lady Luck on your side and can afford to take the odd chance. There are some financial gains possible, and a general push is indicated at work.

5 SATURDAY
Moon Age Day 18   Moon Sign Sagittarius

You can now display great openness and a desire to commit yourself to projects that have been waiting in the wings for a while. This should be a very dynamic phase and one during which you can afford to push your luck a little more than usual. The weekend ought to offer much in the way of potential excitement.

6 SUNDAY
Moon Age Day 19   Moon Sign Sagittarius

The positive trends continue, assisting the Archer to be good to have around at the moment. Although you may decide that the time is right for leisure and pleasure, you still manage to further your intentions at the same time. You can do yourself a lot of good simply by being in the right place at the most opportune time.

7 MONDAY
Moon Age Day 20   Moon Sign Capricorn

You should now be looking forward to ways in which you can broaden your horizons, and the older the year becomes the better in terms of advancement. Even if you don't get everything you want this week, you can get fairly close, and should be able to tap into significant assistance when you need it.

8 TUESDAY
Moon Age Day 21   Moon Sign Capricorn

Beware of disagreements today, and especially ones that are little more than a waste of time. It would be better to avoid getting on the wrong side of anyone if you can, and you might need to be quite giving in order to accommodate the needs of family members. Friends should be easier to deal with under present influences.

9 WEDNESDAY
Moon Age Day 22   Moon Sign Aquarius

The outcome of a major decision made a few weeks ago could now prove to be very rewarding. Your best approach is to keep a sense of proportion at work and do what you can to lift the spirits of anyone who seems a bit down in the dumps. Routines can be quite comfortable, and can help you to live a more ordered sort of day.

10 THURSDAY   *Moon Age Day 23   Moon Sign Aquarius*

You now have what it takes to push ahead on most fronts, and although your powers of concentration are not all they might be, you can elicit a good response under most circumstances. Plan now for things you want to do at the weekend, and make sure that most of these are going to be for pleasure!

11 FRIDAY   *Moon Age Day 24   Moon Sign Pisces*

You may decide to revisit the past in some way today, and this could have to do with relationship issues. Romance is well starred and there are potential gains to be made as far as finances are concerned. Why not catch up on a job you have been promising to do for some time?

12 SATURDAY   *Moon Age Day 25   Moon Sign Pisces*

Trends suggest a restless time for the Archer right now, and that is why it would be best to do something interesting rather than necessary today. You might get a lot from a shopping spree or a visit to somewhere that interests you intellectually. The deeper side of your mind demands attention this weekend.

13 SUNDAY   *Moon Age Day 26   Moon Sign Pisces*

Your strength lies in using your enthusiasm and excitement for projects that capture your imagination. It seems as though you are on the edge of something important but it might be difficult working out exactly what that might be. Friends should be good to have around and may prove to be extremely entertaining.

14 MONDAY   *Moon Age Day 27   Moon Sign Aries*

Do your best to explore the world this week and don't get so bogged down with everyday routines that you fail to notice what is happening around you. Conforming to expectations at work may not be very easy, but this shouldn't matter because it is your spontaneity that appeals to others.

15 TUESDAY   *Moon Age Day 28   Moon Sign Aries*

Present planetary trends assist you to cast your mind far ahead, and many of the actions you are taking now could be for much further down the line. In a moment-by-moment sense you can afford to act on impulse, and you can take advantage of more than a modicum of good luck around you at present.

16 WEDNESDAY   *Moon Age Day 29   Moon Sign Taurus*

The time is right to look out for interesting social encounters and do what you can to mix business with pleasure. You don't take kindly to concentrating every moment on practical matters and work best at the moment when you can show the humorous side of your Sagittarian nature. Your clowning helps you to get yourself noticed.

17 THURSDAY   *Moon Age Day 0   Moon Sign Taurus*

Social trends still look good, and you can get a great deal of joy from all manner of encounters. This is especially true if you are dealing with people who come new to your life. Communications of all kinds prove to be vitally important today, even if they don't seem to be so at first.

18 FRIDAY   *Moon Age Day 1   Moon Sign Gemini*

Getting on side with someone who is in the know could do you a great deal of good. You will have to show the patient side of your nature today when you are dealing with people who seem a bit slow in comparison with your lightning mental processes, but you can still remain kind and as helpful as ever.

19 SATURDAY   *Moon Age Day 2   Moon Sign Gemini*

There's a chance for things to slow down significantly whilst the lunar low is around, and you can't really expect to make much of a spurt for the first part of the weekend. Many Archers will be happy at home today, catching up on domestic tasks and finding time for loved ones, who can be left out somewhat during the week.

20 SUNDAY *Moon Age Day 3 Moon Sign Cancer*

If you are still feeling slightly sluggish, you probably won't have quite the level of enthusiasm or drive that was evident a few days ago. As the day wears on you should begin to feel slightly more optimistic and will be able to give more attention to your partner or sweetheart. You can make this a good day for romance.

21 MONDAY *Moon Age Day 4 Moon Sign Cancer*

You would be wise to retreat a little today but only because you will work best when you are thoughtful and have time to think about things. You can increase the pace of life significantly in the afternoon and during the evening. It might be hard to find the time to put your feet up at any stage towards the end of the day.

22 TUESDAY *Moon Age Day 5 Moon Sign Leo*

Assessing how others are likely to behave under any given circumstance is one of the major skills. This is well accented today and you can make gains by simply knowing which way others are going to turn. It's worth looking towards the needs of your partner at this stage of the week and showing how much you care.

23 WEDNESDAY *Moon Age Day 6 Moon Sign Leo*

With everything to play for today, you have what it takes to turn heads. This is Sagittarius at its social best and there are potential gains available as a result. Your best approach is to avoid unnecessary tasks and stick to what you know is going to further your intentions, especially in a financial sense.

24 THURSDAY *Moon Age Day 7 Moon Sign Virgo*

Monetary security is now to the fore. It could be that you have been spending rather more than you intended recently or simply that the bills are all coming in at the same time. You may decide that getting to grips with the needs of family members should be a priority when work is over.

25 FRIDAY
Moon Age Day 8   Moon Sign Virgo

As the end of the working week approaches you have scope to put something into action that is going to further your intentions next week. In some ways you may now be slightly quieter and more contemplative, and it is possible that someone you mix with most of the time might think you are down in the dumps.

26 SATURDAY
Moon Age Day 9   Moon Sign Virgo

You are in a position to make this a cracking weekend in terms of your personal life. With time to spare you might spend more hours in the company of people you care for and you could also be finding new common interests with the same individuals. Younger family members could give you cause to smile.

27 SUNDAY
Moon Age Day 10   Moon Sign Libra

Look out for new information that comes in today. This might be something to do with the area in which you live or as a result of casual conversations with friends. You can be socially inclined around now, and shouldn't have difficulty getting on well with anyone, even people you don't normally care for.

28 MONDAY
Moon Age Day 11   Moon Sign Libra

Trends inspire an increased desire for travel and for broadening your horizons generally around this time. Active and enterprising, you are able to approach new situations with a great sense of optimism and hope. When it comes to mixing with the world at large you should be showing the very best qualities that the cheerful Archer has to offer.

29 TUESDAY
Moon Age Day 12   Moon Sign Scorpio

You tend to get along well with almost everyone, which is useful at a time when you can get a great deal from those who are in the know. Don't be too surprised if you feel somewhat quieter as the day wears on. The Moon has moved into your solar twelfth house, which often allows a more withdrawn period.

30 WEDNESDAY *Moon Age Day 13 Moon Sign Scorpio*

There are times today when you can get more from life through being willing to stand and wait. It is the natural tendency of the Archer to be moving all the time, but this may not be the case today. Accept that you can think more deeply under present trends and that like everyone else you need to meditate now and again.

31 THURSDAY *Moon Age Day 14 Moon Sign Scorpio*

As today wears on you could find it to be a real mixture. In some ways you want to push the bounds of the possible but at other times you remain essentially locked into your own deeper mind. This is a good time for planning ahead, and particularly so when it comes to fleshing out the details of holidays.

2007

1 FRIDAY
Moon Age Day 15   Moon Sign Sagittarius

The first day of a new month brings with it the lunar high. This offers you a chance to be very excitable, keen to get ahead and lightning in your decision making. Others will need to be very quick to keep up with you, and you have what it takes to be aspiring, inspirational and happy to be of assistance.

2 SATURDAY
Moon Age Day 16   Moon Sign Sagittarius

Yours is a very happy and easy-going sort of zodiac sign, and particularly so when the Moon occupies your zodiac sign. You can make this a weekend to remember by simply following your instincts and by being willing to ring the changes. Any sort of calculated gamble could work out better than might sometimes be the case.

3 SUNDAY
Moon Age Day 17   Moon Sign Capricorn

You feel the need to get along with everyone, and even if you are doing your best to make sure this is the case, not everyone may be equally helpful. You may have to bend over backwards in order to accommodate awkward types, but this is likely to do little to change your basically cheerful frame of mind.

4 MONDAY
Moon Age Day 18   Moon Sign Capricorn

Be prepared to bring a more important social dimension into your life this week. There are some interesting possibilities likely as a result, and the Archer should be right on the ball when it comes to seeing ahead and making the right moves. This could also be a week during which romance figures heavily.

5 TUESDAY *Moon Age Day 19   Moon Sign Aquarius*

The signs are that it is the unusual in life that captivates you today. Anything a little odd or eccentric appeals, and you might even decide to put on your detective hat for some reason. Even casual conversations can set you off down a new road and there are masses of possibilities for new hobbies or pastimes.

6 WEDNESDAY *Moon Age Day 20   Moon Sign Aquarius*

Your personal objectives could be taking a back seat for today, particularly if you are spending most of your time working for others. This is especially true in the case of colleagues, some of whom may be a little out of their depth and need your special touch. Surprising your partner this evening can work wonders!

7 THURSDAY *Moon Age Day 21   Moon Sign Aquarius*

There is a definite lift on offer in the professional sphere, but at the same time you need to be just a little careful because not everyone might be working for your best interests, even if they pretend that they are. There are ways in which everyone can win, and you can now use your Sagittarian know-how to discover them.

8 FRIDAY *Moon Age Day 22   Moon Sign Pisces*

The need for a simpler way forward seems to be emphasised by present trends. It could be that certain matters have become far more complicated than proves to be necessary. Why not slacken the pace a little and take some time out to think things through? A refreshing change at home can be made this evening or across the weekend.

9 SATURDAY *Moon Age Day 23   Moon Sign Pisces*

This Saturday is for you, and you can afford to spend the majority of it doing things that appeal to you personally. This doesn't mean you have to ignore anyone, because you can think up possibilities that suit everyone. You are certainly entering an impulsive phase, but there isn't anything unusual about that.

10 SUNDAY   *Moon Age Day 24   Moon Sign Aries*

A day to open up to loved ones and spill the beans regarding anything that has bothered you for a while. You are now in a position to clear the air and to get on side with those who don't always understand what motivates you. A calmer and more rational period on the home front is indicated by prevailing trends.

11 MONDAY   *Moon Age Day 25   Moon Sign Aries*

With everything to play for as far as your work is concerned, the only possible frustration at the moment is likely to be if those around you cannot keep up with your lightning-quick mental processes. Don't be afraid to explain yourself carefully – it's what people want you to do.

12 TUESDAY   *Moon Age Day 26   Moon Sign Taurus*

There are plenty of good contacts available at the moment, even if these have far more to do with the professional sphere of your life than they have with your personal life. Some frustrations are possible, mainly in the area of love. Avoid doing anything that inspires jealousy in others, and particularly your partner.

13 WEDNESDAY   *Moon Age Day 27   Moon Sign Taurus*

Look out for a few emotional pressures that could be building up thanks to the present position of Mars in your solar chart. You could be slightly snappier than would usually be the case and won't be quite so considerate of the opinions of others. Pointless rules and regulations might also get on your nerves.

14 THURSDAY   *Moon Age Day 28   Moon Sign Gemini*

If things seem quieter now, your best approach is to make the most of it. Knocking your head against a brick wall in your determination to get ahead will only give you a headache. You may as well accept that the lunar low is going to keep life low-key and enjoy the chance for a break.

15 FRIDAY · *Moon Age Day 0 · Moon Sign Gemini*

You would be wise to stick to what you know and don't try anything new or outrageous, at least until tomorrow. You may not have your usual reserves of energy and if you push yourself, your patience will be the first casualty. This would be an excellent time to read a good book and to spend a few hours alone.

16 SATURDAY · *Moon Age Day 1 · Moon Sign Cancer*

Your desire to help others is extremely well marked right now and you have what it takes to get to the heart of a very difficult situation. You should discover your voice again, after a couple of potentially quiet days. When you do speak out, trends suggest it could well be on behalf of the downtrodden.

17 SUNDAY · *Moon Age Day 2 · Moon Sign Cancer*

You can afford to save at least part of this Sunday for yourself, so that you can do things that have been repeatedly put on the shelf for most of this year. If you can, get out into the countryside because the year is advancing fast and you don't want to miss the pleasures it offers. A day to spend time with family members.

18 MONDAY · *Moon Age Day 3 · Moon Sign Leo*

Keep your ears open today because there is some good advice about. The only difficulty here is that to accept what is being suggested, you might need to make a change of direction. This in itself shouldn't be too much of a problem; the question is whether you are willing to eat humble pie!

19 TUESDAY · *Moon Age Day 4 · Moon Sign Leo*

It's possible that those around you might think you lack direction or that the actions you are taking are not sensible. As usual you will want to do what appeals to you and in any case you are aware that it will be impossible to please everyone. A little tact is called for, together with a large slice of patience – something that often eludes you.

20 WEDNESDAY   *Moon Age Day 5   Moon Sign Leo*

Even if you have faith in your own abilities, you might doubt that others have what it takes to keep up. There is a slightly ruthless streak around at the moment and though this isn't entirely unusual for Sagittarius, you do need to exercise a little caution. Major decisions are really best left for a day or two.

21 THURSDAY   *Moon Age Day 6   Moon Sign Virgo*

Today could offer a chance to settle an issue from the past, though you are the one who will have to make the first move. By doing so you could heal a breach that has existed for a long time and can please other family members as a result. Your current strength lies in your 'live and let live' sort of attitude.

22 FRIDAY   *Moon Age Day 7   Moon Sign Virgo*

Emotions run strong and deep at the moment, as is evidenced by the trends of the last few days. It might sometimes be difficult to see where the moves you are about to make will lead, especially in a personal sense. Not everyone might seem to understand you, but if you explain yourself more you can make sure they do.

23 SATURDAY   *Moon Age Day 8   Moon Sign Libra*

Your sunny disposition should now be more in evidence, after a few days during which intensity has reigned. Don't be afraid to cast your mind forward and make interesting plans. This is especially fortunate if there is a trip in the offing. Even today offers the chance of fresh fields and pastures new.

24 SUNDAY   *Moon Age Day 9   Moon Sign Libra*

At the back of your mind there is a little place where excitement is mounting. It may be that you have a plan to do something rather unusual, or the germ of an idea that you just know is going to work out well. It's worth spending some time getting to grips with any family members who seem to be going slightly off the rails.

25 MONDAY   *Moon Age Day 10   Moon Sign Libra*

You can get on especially well today in situations that demand your full attention and your excellent ability to get a message across. In work situations you have the ability to lead from the front and should not expect anyone to do anything you are not capable of doing yourself. Rules are important today, but not if they restrict you.

26 TUESDAY   *Moon Age Day 11   Moon Sign Scorpio*

Trends incline you to be more sensitive than usual to the casual remarks that are being made around you. Before you fly off the handle, you would be wise to make sure that these comments are definitely aimed in your direction. The Archer can be just a little cranky at the moment and apt to be slightly irrational.

27 WEDNESDAY   *Moon Age Day 12   Moon Sign Scorpio*

A quieter day is possible, but at least this gives you the chance to catch up with yourself. It might seem as if everyone else is getting ahead, whilst you have to sit around and watch. Don't worry because you can reverse this situation quickly enough tomorrow, when the lunar high comes to your aid.

28 THURSDAY   *Moon Age Day 13   Moon Sign Sagittarius*

Influences come together today to offer you a more satisfying and happy sort of day. Actually, much of what happens is down to your own actions, but is definitely assisted by the lunar high. You can afford to push your luck a little, but there is nothing too unusual about that!

29 FRIDAY   *Moon Age Day 14   Moon Sign Sagittarius*

Social interaction is favoured, and you can use today to persuade someone that your plans for the future are the most viable. This shouldn't be too difficult because your natural ability to sell yourself is stronger than ever. It might now be possible to please almost everyone, whilst at the same time enjoying the ride yourself.

30 SATURDAY   *Moon Age Day 15   Moon Sign Capricorn*

It is towards the practical aspects of life that trends encourage you to turn your mind this weekend, and you could be busy around the homestead, getting things sorted out to your satisfaction. You might have to make a few new starts, but the achievements that are possible as a result make the effort worthwhile.

July

2007

1 SUNDAY ☿ *Moon Age Day 16   Moon Sign Capricorn*

The first day of July offers an opportunity to coast along on what can be a generally contented sort of Sunday. If the time is your own, it's worth thinking up something you know is going to be welcomed by family members and also finding a few moments to address the needs of your partner especially.

2 MONDAY ☿ *Moon Age Day 17   Moon Sign Capricorn*

There are signs that not everything that happens at the start of this week may be working to your advantage, though you need to be careful because you can be wrong. Even if others seem to be working against your best interests, it is possible that they genuinely do know better than you do.

3 TUESDAY ☿ *Moon Age Day 18   Moon Sign Aquarius*

If you allow yourself to become irritated today over things that are not of any real importance, the only real loser is going to be you. Right now you are inclined to be like a terrier with a rag and will chase your notions so far they become ludicrous. Be prepared to settle down and accept that some things are simply the way they are.

4 WEDNESDAY ☿ *Moon Age Day 19   Moon Sign Aquarius*

New opportunities for employment are a distinct possibility. Some Archers may be thinking in terms of an entirely new start or an alteration with regard to present responsibilities. The focus is on sharing warmth and understanding with friends, and it is possible that a friendship could become much deeper for a few Sagittarians.

5 THURSDAY   ☿   *Moon Age Day 20   Moon Sign Pisces*

With a continually greater sense of personal freedom, you may not take kindly to being told what you have to do. This goes to the heart of your basic motivations because Sagittarius does not make a good hostage to fortune. On a more pleasant note, today offers you scope to strengthen your position in a financial sense.

6 FRIDAY   ☿   *Moon Age Day 21   Moon Sign Pisces*

You have what it takes to show considerable personal charm today when it matters the most and can get most of what you want simply by speaking the right words. You can make sure most people respond to your approach and that they go to great lengths to make you happy. Repaying this kindness is not at all difficult.

7 SATURDAY   ☿   *Moon Age Day 22   Moon Sign Aries*

In the roller-coaster fashion that is typical of your life at the moment, the very same people you got on so well with yesterday could present you with problems right now. The fact is that you may once again be feeling tied down and unable to make the moves that suit you. Why not stop and think things through before moving on?

8 SUNDAY   ☿   *Moon Age Day 23   Moon Sign Aries*

It is towards the really original side of your nature that you are encouraged to turn today to discover the best way forward. Sagittarius can be very creative at present, and you may decide to embark upon specific changes at home that are going to make you feel more comfortable with your lot in life generally.

9 MONDAY   ☿   *Moon Age Day 24   Moon Sign Taurus*

Since you identify strongly today with the aims and intentions of others, you can make sure this is a day for sharing. Not that there is anything remotely unusual about this for Sagittarius. You get the most out of life when co-operating, and can now elicit some real favours from others.

10 TUESDAY   ☿   *Moon Age Day 25   Moon Sign Taurus*

At this time you work best when you are able to make your own decisions, and you could feel just slightly restricted if messages from above restrict your actions in any way. With everything to play for in a romantic sense you should be able to pep up your love life no end, maybe by springing a surprise.

11 WEDNESDAY   *Moon Age Day 26   Moon Sign Gemini*

Things have potential to be quieter today, mainly in response to the lunar low. This is a time best spent planning rather than doing, and you can also develop all sorts of ideas for the future. Don't allow yourself to become depressed over issues that under normal circumstances would hardly cross your mind.

12 THURSDAY   *Moon Age Day 27   Moon Sign Gemini*

If you are still not on top form, you may well be quite happy to potter along quietly and even to stay in the background more than would usually be the case. Beware of allowing a sense of impending disaster to permeate your life, since it could prompt you to take actions that are really not necessary. Try to remain optimistic.

13 FRIDAY   *Moon Age Day 28   Moon Sign Cancer*

What you are able to bring to your life now the lunar low is out of the way is a greater sense of purpose and significantly more concentration. Breaking down barriers comes as second nature to you, and particularly so under present planetary trends. Routines might seem comfortable, but could be restricting.

14 SATURDAY   *Moon Age Day 29   Moon Sign Cancer*

It is in the company of others that you have scope to make your best progress now. This is not the best time to be going it alone because you will probably have to work that much harder without the support of colleagues and friends. You should be able to make sure that any worries regarding family members don't last for very long.

15 SUNDAY
Moon Age Day 0   Moon Sign Cancer

There are signs that people who haven't figured in your life so far this year are likely to make a return visit. It may be that someone from far away is appearing or else you remember an individual who has been on the periphery of your life recently. Your attitude towards family matters might be seen as rather unusual now.

16 MONDAY
Moon Age Day 1   Moon Sign Leo

Beware of being too rash, especially when it comes to spending money. You have a genuine thirst for pleasure and luxury around now and will need to curb your spending somewhat if you are not to count the cost later. Ask yourself whether a planned new purchase is at all necessary.

17 TUESDAY
Moon Age Day 2   Moon Sign Leo

This would be a good time to fix your attention on the medium and long term and to think up new strategies that could see you better off than has been the case of late. Friends should come good with their promises and can be a source of timely assistance. Romance can become a more significant factor as the week advances.

18 WEDNESDAY
Moon Age Day 3   Moon Sign Virgo

The more you set out to have a good time, the greater is the enjoyment you can bring into your life. This is not a good period during which to concentrate only on work, and you will be at your best when there is always something to which you can look forward. A day to avoid dull and uninspiring types.

19 THURSDAY
Moon Age Day 4   Moon Sign Virgo

Don't overlook those little details that can mean all the difference to your ultimate success. This is especially true at work but the trend also spills over into your home life. It is the apparently inconsequential matters that need most concentration and which can assure you of getting on well for the next few days.

20 FRIDAY
Moon Age Day 5   Moon Sign Libra

You have what it takes to be extremely diplomatic whilst the Moon is in Libra and should be able to get on especially well with those born under the three Air signs of Gemini, Libra and Aquarius. From a monetary point of view it would be wise to remember that not all that glistens turns out to be made of gold.

21 SATURDAY
Moon Age Day 6   Moon Sign Libra

By all means stand by the decisions you have made, but not to the point that it becomes necessary to fall out with anyone. If you need to make slight alterations in order to keep the peace, then that's the way it has to be. There might be some frustration caused by altered plans, but at least you should remain popular.

22 SUNDAY
Moon Age Day 7   Moon Sign Libra

It is towards your home that your mind is encouraged to turn today. Even if you are still as keen as ever to enjoy yourself, the needs of family members may well predominate. This is no bad thing, because you lead such a busy life that you don't always spend as much time considering loved ones as you might.

23 MONDAY
Moon Age Day 8   Moon Sign Scorpio

You may feel slightly frustrated by the actions and opinions of others today, but the real problem is that the Moon has moved into your solar twelfth house. This could make you less able to react quickly and more inclined to settle for second-best. A day to find pleasure in small things and in personal attachments.

24 TUESDAY
Moon Age Day 9   Moon Sign Scorpio

This has potential to be a quiet day when you are less willing to exercise your power to change anything at all. It is very unusual for the Archer to be totally withdrawn from society and events, but that's the way things may have to be for just a few hours. Don't worry because there are much better times available almost immediately.

25 WEDNESDAY *Moon Age Day 10   Moon Sign Sagittarius*

Talk about sudden reversals! Where life seemed dull, you can now make it very exciting and you could be filled with enthusiasm from the moment you get out of bed. Getting things right first time seems important and should not be at all difficult under present trends. It's worth avoiding unnecessary routines and details.

26 THURSDAY   *Moon Age Day 11   Moon Sign Sagittarius*

You can still be on top form, and shouldn't have any problem letting others know what you want. Whether they have what it takes to keep up with your quick thinking remains to be seen, but you can also be fairly patient and willing to spend whatever time is necessary coaching those with whom you work and live.

27 FRIDAY   *Moon Age Day 12   Moon Sign Sagittarius*

For the third day in a row the Moon remains in your zodiac sign, assisting you to fire on all cylinders. Keeping a sense of proportion could be difficult, but you may decide it isn't necessary in any case under present trends. A time to let your plans be big and worry later about how to make them into realities.

28 SATURDAY   *Moon Age Day 13   Moon Sign Capricorn*

You can make sure that what goes on around you at home is heart-warming and more than interesting. For this reason alone you could be abandoning any thought of real practical progress today and may be spending most of your time concerned with family matters. A shopping spree might also be good.

29 SUNDAY   *Moon Age Day 14   Moon Sign Capricorn*

There are a few pitfalls around today and these come mainly from the difficulty of second-guessing the actions and motivations of those around you. Maybe you are not concentrating as much as would normally be the case, and you probably don't have much in the way of intuition for the moment.

30 MONDAY   *Moon Age Day 15   Moon Sign Aquarius*

With a better day in prospect and a week of possibilities before you, today responds best if you start positively and keeep busy. Beware of getting bogged down with issues that are of no real importance, and where possible allow others to take some of the strain and to tackle less interesting jobs.

31 TUESDAY   *Moon Age Day 16   Moon Sign Aquarius*

It is the emotional side of life that is highlighted right now. If you sense your partner is less than happy about something, be prepared to have a serious talk at some stage to sort things out. If you have been looking for new love, this is a day to keep your eyes open.

2007

1 WEDNESDAY
Moon Age Day 17   Moon Sign Pisces

The first day of a new month offers a happy and generally carefree interlude. The hot month of August has come along and you may have your mind set on travel. If holidays are in the offing you need to deal with all those last-minute details, like making sure you have all the suntan lotion you will need!

2 THURSDAY
Moon Age Day 18   Moon Sign Pisces

The Archer can show itself to be quite selfless today, and much of what you do is for the direct benefit of others. If your social conscience is aroused, you could be dealing with some issues that have to do with the area in which you live and with local politics. Trends suggest that you can be quite argumentative right now.

3 FRIDAY
Moon Age Day 19   Moon Sign Aries

What seemed like a good idea at the time may be less so in the cold light of dawn. There is a distinct possibility that you will have to re-track over specific issues and to think on your feet. Fortunately there is nothing difficult about this for the average Archer, and you should revel in the need to make up your mind quickly.

4 SATURDAY
Moon Age Day 20   Moon Sign Aries

Your sense of fair play is once again much emphasised, and you can use this to be very protective in the case of family members and friends. You can make the weekend a happy one, with plenty to keep you busy and a search for enjoyment, no matter what you are doing or who you do it with.

5 SUNDAY
Moon Age Day 21   Moon Sign Taurus

It's worth keeping your ears open today in case you hear things that can be turned to your advantage. Half an idea from someone else could be turned into something magnificent if you apply yourself to it. You can best avoid dull patches by ringing the changes and by getting out of the house at some stage.

6 MONDAY
Moon Age Day 22   Moon Sign Taurus

Material concerns count for a great deal at the beginning of this week, and your strength lies in getting things done, even if others prove a little tardy in keeping up. Later in the day you may run out of steam, particularly if you are trying to achieve too much.

7 TUESDAY
Moon Age Day 23   Moon Sign Taurus

Why not do something today that pleases you? For the last week or two you have been encouraged to put yourself out for others, and now it is time to be just a little selfish. Actually this probably isn't entirely true because you have what it takes to think up strategies that still keep those around you happy.

8 WEDNESDAY
Moon Age Day 24   Moon Sign Gemini

Once again there are signs that you are on the go from morning until night, but now you might have a little fatigue to deal with. This comes along courtesy of the lunar low and you would be well advised to let your friends and colleagues take some of the strain. The best way to deal with today is to take a well-earned rest.

9 THURSDAY
Moon Age Day 25   Moon Sign Gemini

You may not be making all the progress you would wish at the moment, particularly if minor frustrations come along all the time to stop you in your tracks. Instead of getting upset about these it would be sensible to clear the decks for actions that come later, whilst for now you can act more as an observer than a doer.

10 FRIDAY
Moon Age Day 26   Moon Sign Cancer

What's this – Sagittarius being socially reluctant? Your friendly side is not as pronounced as would normally be the case, and the stupidity of certain other people could really get on your nerves. You won't want to show the fact and there are times today when your best response is simply to count to ten.

11 SATURDAY
Moon Age Day 27   Moon Sign Cancer

You should be able to get more or less back to normal now and enjoy all the benefits that are available at this time of year. Not least amongst these is the warmer weather and the longer days. What a great time this would be for a barbecue or some other form of open-air get-together with friends.

12 SUNDAY
Moon Age Day 28   Moon Sign Leo

Stand by for a fairly smooth-running sort of day, but not a period during which finances are necessarily very strong. This shouldn't matter too much because the sort of things that interest you at the moment are unlikely to cost you very much. It's worth keeping a sense of proportion regarding any minor spats in the family.

13 MONDAY
Moon Age Day 0   Moon Sign Leo

New ideas and fresh starts seem to be the order of the day. Avoid pointless routines and concentrate on matters that please you personally. Beware of acting too much on impulse, even though this is a tall order for the Archer. The more organised you are now, the better you play into the hands of present astrological trends.

14 TUESDAY
Moon Age Day 1   Moon Sign Virgo

You may well be turning towards pet projects today and will be quite happy to potter along steadily. There may be sight complications in family matters or in discussions with colleagues. Gains can be made by remaining steadfast, but not to the point that you become too fixed in your attitude.

15 WEDNESDAY   *Moon Age Day 2   Moon Sign Virgo*

There are trends around today that favour financial prosperity, and you can use these to make sure you are slightly better off than you may have expected at this time of the month. It could be that you are simply proving to be luckier than usual, but it is also possible that something you did in the past now begins to pay dividends.

16 THURSDAY   *Moon Age Day 3   Moon Sign Virgo*

Communication is positively highlighted at this time and you can get more or less anything you want by simply asking in the right way. At the same time, progress is a definite possibility in romance, especially in the case of Archers who have recently found a new love.

17 FRIDAY   *Moon Age Day 4   Moon Sign Libra*

Even if there are many challenges around today, this can be a very positive thing as far as you are concerned and simply brings new incentives when they prove to be most welcome. Don't get too obsessed with details, especially at work, because it is an overview of life that matters the most at the moment.

18 SATURDAY   *Moon Age Day 5   Moon Sign Libra*

Energy should be used sparingly today, not because there is any lack of it but because concentration brings its own rewards. You have what it takes to instinctively understand the thoughts and motivations of others, and can also afford to offer timely assistance to family members and friends.

19 SUNDAY   *Moon Age Day 6   Moon Sign Scorpio*

Your desire to know things and to increase your level of expertise is to the fore at present. You can drink in the world like a cold lager on a hot day, and shouldn't be at all put off simply because there isn't always the amount of personal support around you would wish. Creative potential is especially favoured now.

20 MONDAY
Moon Age Day 7   Moon Sign Scorpio

This could be a slightly quieter day, as the Moon passes through your solar twelfth house. You can use the time to contemplate matters and to look at life in a more detached manner than is sometimes the case for the Archer. Why not put a little more effort into making sure family members are content with their lot?

21 TUESDAY
Moon Age Day 8   Moon Sign Scorpio

Another fairly steady day is there for the taking, offering you more hours than usual to observe situations. This could turn out to be a very positive thing because by tomorrow the lunar high comes along. All your considered opinions and general homework should prove to be very useful during the middle of the week.

22 WEDNESDAY
Moon Age Day 9   Moon Sign Sagittarius

You can make yourself the centre of attention today and get well up to speed in most matters. Confidence is high and this could prove to be the luckiest day of August as far as you are concerned. What shines out most is your personality, which you can make sure that everyone notices and most people love!

23 THURSDAY
Moon Age Day 10   Moon Sign Sagittarius

Don't hold back today. This is 'your' time of the month and a period during which you need to put your ideas across with enthusiasm and a sense of personal certainty. The more confident you appear, the greater is the likelihood that things will go your way. Self-belief is absolutely everything to Sagittarius now.

24 FRIDAY
Moon Age Day 11   Moon Sign Capricorn

Your strength lies in your great sense of personal rejuvenation around now and you should be quite willing to turn your world upside down if that is what it takes to get your way. If the same cannot be said for those with whom you live, a little understanding on your part would be welcome.

25 SATURDAY   *Moon Age Day 12   Moon Sign Capricorn*

Even if your drive to achieve is still strong, you may not have quite the level of follow-through that was the case earlier in the week. Nevertheless you can make this a good weekend and should be quite happy to go with the flow in social situations. Sagittarius is encouraged to be physically active now.

26 SUNDAY   *Moon Age Day 13   Moon Sign Aquarius*

Some care would be sensible with regard to specific decisions, and especially ones that have a personal or a romantic dimension. You may decide to spend the day with loved ones if you can and to allow the traces of responsibility to fall for just a few hours. Your demonstrations of affection should be most welcome.

27 MONDAY   *Moon Age Day 14   Moon Sign Aquarius*

Even if you can't get all your own way at the start of this week, that shouldn't matter because you are in such a good frame of mind that you probably won't care too much. If work is piling up you will need to apply yourself, but be prepared to look for ways in which you can get others to take some of the strain.

28 TUESDAY   *Moon Age Day 15   Moon Sign Aquarius*

You might be slightly preoccupied with the past for a day or two, which is fairly unusual for your zodiac sign. There's nothing wrong with this, except the realisation on your part that what really matters is the present and the future. Some small frustrations are possible later on.

29 WEDNESDAY   *Moon Age Day 16   Moon Sign Pisces*

Expect a sort of split in your thinking now. Whilst you tend to dwell on matters in some ways, in others you are full of beans and anxious to get on. Others may find it difficult to follow what is a slightly mercurial attitude on your part and they may accuse you of being too changeable.

30 THURSDAY   *Moon Age Day 17   Moon Sign Pisces*

You may not be expressing yourself quite as clearly as you would
wish, though this may have little to do with you personally and is
more a reflection of the fact that some people simply are not
listening. If you have to repeat yourself too many times you could
easily get cranky.

31 FRIDAY   *Moon Age Day 18   Moon Sign Aries*

Freedom is the best key to happiness as the working week comes to
an end. Even if there is little you can do about this during the day,
by the time the evening arrives you should be prepared to get out
and have some fun. Avoid piling yourself up with unnecessary jobs,
either today or across the weekend.

September
2007

1 SATURDAY
Moon Age Day 19   Moon Sign Aries

Life needs to be an open book for you right now. Today responds best if you leave aside all complications and keep things just as simple as you can. In your approach to others you need to be honest. If you are, they will understand you instantly and misunderstandings shouldn't occur. This is a good day for making major purchases.

2 SUNDAY
Moon Age Day 20   Moon Sign Taurus

On the whole you have what it takes to show yourself to be friendly and extremely charming today. There is a definite need for action of some sort and you would not take kindly to being stuck indoors throughout the day. Get out to the coast or the country and if the weather is good, take a picnic. Enjoyment is everything now.

3 MONDAY
Moon Age Day 21   Moon Sign Taurus

Make the most of today because things may well get quieter until after the middle of the week. If you get a good start now, you can cruise through Tuesday and Wednesday. Look for new social possibilities for later in the day and maybe think about getting involved in sport.

4 TUESDAY
Moon Age Day 22   Moon Sign Gemini

It's worth letting those around you do most of the work today whilst you adopt a supervisory role. It's time to call in a few favours and if you do the lunar low shouldn't be half so difficult to deal with. Just remember that this is not an ideal day to push your luck or to make assumptions about almost anything.

5 WEDNESDAY   *Moon Age Day 23   Moon Sign Gemini*

This could be another less than satisfying sort of day, but it really depends what you expect of yourself. If you keep yourself to yourself more than usual and avoid getting involved in decision making for the moment, all should be well. By the evening you may simply decide to put your feet up.

6 THURSDAY   *Moon Age Day 24   Moon Sign Cancer*

You now have scope to change things for the better. Although you could still have some slight difficulty getting your ideas across to others, you clearly know your own business well and can forge ahead in at least one direction. Maybe it would be best to curb your natural enthusiasm, at least until tomorrow.

7 FRIDAY   *Moon Age Day 25   Moon Sign Cancer*

You may have a few doubts about people who appear to know everything about a particular subject, and might even decide to do some investigating for yourself. If you need some warmth and solace, why not approach some friends? Spending some time with a really good pal can work wonders.

8 SATURDAY   *Moon Age Day 26   Moon Sign Leo*

Your sensitivity is honed to perfection under present planetary trends, and you shouldn't have any trouble seeing into the lives of those around you. You are now far less likely to tread on anyone's toes, and on the contrary you have what it takes to make your colleagues and friends feel extremely comfortable.

9 SUNDAY   *Moon Age Day 27   Moon Sign Leo*

There are signs that you may be coming to the end of a particular phase of your life, and the time is right to look ahead for something new. This is unlikely to have a bearing on relationships and seems to be an entirely practical matter. A day to sort out your finances and get all those bits of paper into some sort of order.

10 MONDAY
Moon Age Day 28   Moon Sign Leo

Being organised and practical is fine, but that doesn't necessarily mean you are enjoying yourself. Certain aspects of life can be something of a chore now, and what you need is some sort of diversion. Don't keep pushing and pushing with regard to an issues that would work better if you simply waited a while.

11 TUESDAY
Moon Age Day 29   Moon Sign Virgo

You may not have your usual ability to deal with practical matters in an efficient way, which is why you might decide to call on the good offices of someone in the know. This is not necessarily a bad thing because you can make sure you go up in the estimation of a superior, especially if you show that you are willing to learn.

12 WEDNESDAY
Moon Age Day 0   Moon Sign Virgo

Confidence is potentially higher today, motivating you to rise into the mainstream of life once again. Romance looks especially well starred under present trends, and those amongst you who have just started a new relationship can make sure that it is blossoming. Support can be gained from family members.

13 THURSDAY
Moon Age Day 1   Moon Sign Libra

What you show more than anything today is a tendency to be resourceful. You should know what you want from life and have some very good ideas about how you can get it. Beware of being too quick to tell someone else they are wrong. A little diplomacy works better, no matter how sure you are of yourself.

14 FRIDAY
Moon Age Day 2   Moon Sign Libra

Mental pursuits are now well accented, and that quick mind of yours can be put to work in a hundred different ways. Your anger could easily be aroused by strangers behaving in a stupid way, but you shouldn't have much trouble with friends, most of whom you can persuade to be very co-operative.

15 SATURDAY   *Moon Age Day 3   Moon Sign Scorpio*

Just being what you naturally are should be enough to get you noticed right now. There may be some slight difficulties across the weekend, but these are likely to be caused by the insensitivity of others, mainly family members. Don't be surprised if you are called upon to sort out a dispute that you see as being entirely stupid.

16 SUNDAY   *Moon Age Day 4   Moon Sign Scorpio*

It's worth spending some time at home because you have a potentially busy week in front of you and will gain significantly if you are well rested. The advancing year already shows signs that autumn in coming, and you may decide to busy yourself in your house or garden, getting things tidied up to your satisfaction.

17 MONDAY   *Moon Age Day 5   Moon Sign Scorpio*

There are influences around now that definitely help you to quicken your mind and which find you well able to address issues that could have confused you in the past. Energy levels could well be increasing and you shouldn't have much difficulty dealing with anyone who has given you problems in the past.

18 TUESDAY   *Moon Age Day 6   Moon Sign Sagittarius*

You can be both magnetic and dynamic today and should be quite happy to put yourself out there in the social mainstream of life. There is something distinctly dramatic about your nature at the moment and you could be approaching certain situations in a very stage-like way. It looks as though Sagittarius the poser is putting in an appearance!

19 WEDNESDAY   *Moon Age Day 7   Moon Sign Sagittarius*

Not everyone can keep up with your thought processes as the lunar high continues, and you may have to keep slowing down in order to accommodate colleagues. You would be in a good position to impress a boss but you should avoid giving the impression that you know everything – even if you are sure you do.

131

20 THURSDAY   *Moon Age Day 8   Moon Sign Capricorn*

There are signs that not everything in the garden is looking rosy. There may be slight hiccups in personal attachments, especially if you have not been quite as attentive as you should have been. Why not put matters right with a kind word, a romantic text message or perhaps even a timely bunch of flowers?

21 FRIDAY   *Moon Age Day 9   Moon Sign Capricorn*

All types of travel, together with cultural diversions, can help you to lift the quality of your Friday. Things can happen very quickly at the moment, but thinking on your feet should be second nature, and doesn't give you any real problem. There could be slight financial gains to be made, maybe as a result of simple good luck.

22 SATURDAY   *Moon Age Day 10   Moon Sign Capricorn*

Your will-power is legendary, and there are few people around at the moment who can match you in anything, at least not once you have really made up your mind. Beware of being too quick to criticise people in the family or amongst good friends. Someone else may leap to their defence and cause you real problems.

23 SUNDAY   *Moon Age Day 11   Moon Sign Aquarius*

Your strengths are now to the fore, even if there is no real way to prove the fact on a Sunday. Instead of worrying about professional matters, you may decide to turn your attention to sorting things out in a family and a personal sense. In any sort of sport you have potential to be on a winning streak now.

24 MONDAY   *Moon Age Day 12   Moon Sign Aquarius*

There is a strong emphasis on financial security, and you would be wise to count the pennies today, even if it is not necessary to do so. There is a positive side to this because you can get some real bargains if you are willing to look around and to barter. Your general attitude should motivate others to approach you in a fair way.

25 TUESDAY
Moon Age Day 13   Moon Sign Pisces

There is no alternative to experience when it comes to getting ahead today, and you would be well advised to concentrate on what you know the best. You have what it takes to turn heads in any social setting and you also retain a good ability to mix business with pleasure to your distinct advantage.

26 WEDNESDAY
Moon Age Day 14   Moon Sign Pisces

Everyday affairs should be looking generally settled, but if there is nothing especially exciting going on you have scope to do something about the fact yourself. If it seems that one particular task is taking forever, you could get it out of the way quicker if you enlist some help.

27 THURSDAY
Moon Age Day 15   Moon Sign Aries

The Sun is now in a very strong position to offer you more in the way of deep contentment, and for the next few weeks you ought to be quite settled inside yourself. Not that everything is exactly the way you want it to be. If that were the case, you would hardly be typical of your Sagittarian birth sign.

28 FRIDAY
Moon Age Day 16   Moon Sign Aries

If you decide to make a push for even greater freedom today, you could get on the wrong side of others as a result. The best way forward is to show a greater understanding of those around you and not to cross them simply for the sake of it. The Archer can sometimes be an unintentional bully.

29 SATURDAY
Moon Age Day 17   Moon Sign Taurus

If there is something really important at the back of your mind you may choose today to explore it more fully. In some ways you are now much more organised and want to pigeonhole everything if you can. That's fine for you, but will it suit everyone else? Once again a little diplomacy is called for.

30 SUNDAY
Moon Age Day 18   Moon Sign Taurus

The present planetary picture offers every opportunity for personal rewards, which is why you can afford to chance your arm more than usual. Beware of red tape and small print, particularly in connection with family affairs.

October 2007

1 MONDAY
Moon Age Day 19   Moon Sign Gemini

It's the start of a new month and there is everything to play for in both the professional and the personal stakes. The trouble is that the lunar low heralds a more lethargic interlude, and you may be less inclined to stick your neck out. There is little point in fighting this because you may well keep making mistakes.

2 TUESDAY
Moon Age Day 20   Moon Sign Gemini

This might be another less than inspiring day, which is why you may decide to spend time on your own. You could feel just slightly depressed though if so you need to tell yourself that you know this is just a small hiccup and that everything will seem better by tomorrow. Be prepared to keep up your efforts on behalf of a younger person.

3 WEDNESDAY
Moon Age Day 21   Moon Sign Cancer

In a social sense you need change, and if it doesn't seem to come along of its own volition you can change things by your own actions. In some ways your mind may now be committed to the past, which can bring warm memories but not much in the way of practical help. It's worth keeping your mind on the future when you can.

4 THURSDAY
Moon Age Day 22   Moon Sign Cancer

Conflicts can arise today, particularly if you are not in tune with the ideas of colleagues or maybe even friends. If a specific issue threatens to spoil the peace, why not ask yourself if your point of view is valid? Even if it is, you need to question whether it is really important. You can afford to allow someone else the laurels this time.

135

5 FRIDAY
Moon Age Day 23   Moon Sign Leo

It might be sensible to look closely at family finances. It isn't very long until Christmas, and if you do some judicious spending right now you could save some money in the longer term. It is the essence of your nature at the moment to look well ahead and to be filled with exciting plans.

6 SATURDAY
Moon Age Day 24   Moon Sign Leo

A day to grasp opportunities as and when they arise, especially in a social sense. There might even be some offers for outings or social gatherings this weekend that come along at the last minute. If you can possible rearrange things to accommodate them, you will probably be pleased that you did.

7 SUNDAY
Moon Age Day 25   Moon Sign Leo

If at all possible you need to put a full stop to a particular issue that has been on your mind for a while now. The planets are in the right position for you to make new starts and to look at situations with a very new attitude. A day to spend some time with your partner and enjoy what romance has to offer at this fortunate time.

8 MONDAY
Moon Age Day 26   Moon Sign Virgo

New and helpful relationships are now a possibility. Be prepared to take what you can from them, especially in practical matters. There are some unexpected gains available at the moment, but it isn't like the Archer to stick fast, and whilst others are thinking about things you should be making maximum advantage.

9 TUESDAY
Moon Age Day 27   Moon Sign Virgo

You would be wise to exercise a little sense where money is concerned and to avoid spending lavishly on things you don't really need at all. There are some gains possible in terms of your romantic life, but these tend to come despite you rather than because of you. You can afford to take benefits where they are offered and not to question them.

10 WEDNESDAY   *Moon Age Day 28   Moon Sign Libra*

Get started with new projects today and make the most of the positive planetary trends that surround you. This would be an ideal time to contact anyone who can help you to complete a job that has been waiting in the wings for quite some time. Your resourcefulness knows no bounds under present influences.

11 THURSDAY   *Moon Age Day 0   Moon Sign Libra*

Your intuition is heightened around now and you should not turn away from those important little messages that crop up at the back of your mind. You should know instinctively who you can trust and who should be left alone. Following the advice of a friend can assist you to make a small financial gain.

12 FRIDAY   ☿   *Moon Age Day 1   Moon Sign Libra*

If you make sure you are in the know regarding your own finances, you should be able to turn your mind towards specific investments that are going to be of use to you in the longer-term future. Sagittarians are usually people of the present moment, but you do have greater patience now and a willingness to wait.

13 SATURDAY   ☿   *Moon Age Day 2   Moon Sign Scorpio*

Things may quieten down for the weekend, so you could well decide not to push yourself too hard. With the Moon in your solar twelfth house you have scope to be planning rather than doing, and you should also be making the most of positive family trends and pleasant friendship encounters.

14 SUNDAY   ☿   *Moon Age Day 3   Moon Sign Scorpio*

Your sense of what looks and feels right is enhanced, even if you are slightly less willing than usual to put yourself fully on display. It's worth using at least part of today to plan for the new working week that lies ahead. If you are between jobs at present this would be an excellent time to really look around.

15 MONDAY ☿ *Moon Age Day 4   Moon Sign Sagittarius*

This has potential to be an impulsive and energetic day. The lunar high coincides with the start of a new working week and brings with it plenty of opportunities. Even if not everyone is on your side, it doesn't really matter because you can plough on regardless. At work actions speak louder than words.

16 TUESDAY ☿ *Moon Age Day 5   Moon Sign Sagittarius*

Another good day can be achieved, and you will have everything you need to turn ideas into actions. If there is the slightest possibility of movement in your life, for example some sort of journey, this needs to be grasped firmly with both hands. You might have volunteered today before you even realise!

17 WEDNESDAY ☿ *Moon Age Day 6   Moon Sign Sagittarius*

For the third day in a row you have the ability to get the bit between your teeth. Nothing and nobody should be able to prevent your forward motion in life – unless of course you deliberately allow them to do so. You please yourself, and hard luck to anyone who thinks they are the master of the Archer!

18 THURSDAY ☿ *Moon Age Day 7   Moon Sign Capricorn*

There are further rewards possible in the financial sphere, and you have what you need to get ahead in terms of your work. If there is any fly in the ointment at the moment it might come from family members, particularly any who seem to be less than happy with their lot and are expressing the fact.

19 FRIDAY ☿ *Moon Age Day 8   Moon Sign Capricorn*

Do be ready to make allowances for others today, especially if you can't really proceed without them. This could mean having to slow down in order to let colleagues catch up. At home you may be less responsive to the general needs of loved ones, and particularly your partner.

20 SATURDAY ☿ *Moon Age Day 9* *Moon Sign Aquarius*

New incentives look positive, but you may find you are inclined to be slightly lazier than usual. What might really appeal to you is luxury in one form or another, and it is possible that under present trends you don't mind at all being pampered. In a social sense you have what it takes to look and feel right, which is how you can get noticed.

21 SUNDAY ☿ *Moon Age Day 10* *Moon Sign Aquarius*

With your intuition working strongly at the moment you can afford to take more notice of that little voice at the back of your mind. You needn't be held back by those who say you can't do something. In any case this could be like a red rag to a bull, because it makes you even more inclined to try.

22 MONDAY ☿ *Moon Age Day 11* *Moon Sign Pisces*

Your thinking powers are much intensified today, and you may spend more time mulling things over than you do applying yourself. This is not necessarily a bad thing because there are periods during which you need to batter your ideas into shape before you get going in a concrete sense. You can take action a little further down the road.

23 TUESDAY ☿ *Moon Age Day 12* *Moon Sign Pisces*

When it comes to getting on well with people who matter, you can now be right on the ball. Little Mercury is especially helpful to you at this time and assists you to communicate with lots of different sorts of people, without really having to think too much. Your power to sell an idea should be stronger than ever.

24 WEDNESDAY ☿ *Moon Age Day 13* *Moon Sign Pisces*

Even common or garden routines can seem more interesting under present trends, and you can undertake menial tasks with a greater willingness. What seems to appeal to you most today is not so much what you do, but how you do it. Your general view should be a longer-term one during the remainder of this month.

25 THURSDAY ☿ *Moon Age Day 14 Moon Sign Aries*

This is a time during which it ought to be easy for you to get others round to your way of thinking. By all means take some time out to persuade and debate, but don't let this go on for too long. At the end of the day you have to follow your own lead, even if this means going it alone on a few occasions.

26 FRIDAY ☿ *Moon Age Day 15 Moon Sign Aries*

There can be significant difference of opinion around, and you might simply have to agree to differ. This is certainly better than arguing. Under present trends little or nothing is gained by falling out with anyone, and this is especially true at work. Why not spend some time in the evening doing just what takes your fancy?

27 SATURDAY ☿ *Moon Age Day 16 Moon Sign Taurus*

Trends suggest that it would be all too easy at the moment to wear yourself out before you have even started a task. Your mind is now inclined to work overtime and even when you are sleeping you may be mulling things over. There is a slightly obsessive quality to the Sagittarian mind, and it is highlighted at present.

28 SUNDAY ☿ *Moon Age Day 17 Moon Sign Taurus*

If you want to enjoy personal rewards today, don't be afraid to put in that extra bit of effort that can make all the difference. The signs are that you are right at the edge of something very important. All that is required now is the final push, plus a belief in your own intuition and ideas.

29 MONDAY ☿ *Moon Age Day 18 Moon Sign Gemini*

This may not be the most dynamic start to a new week that you have ever encountered. The lunar low does nothing to boost your resolve or your energy, and you may decide it is easier to watch than to take part. This trend only lasts a couple of days, and if you do push yourself too hard you could make mistakes and have to start again.

30 TUESDAY ☿ *Moon Age Day 19   Moon Sign Gemini*

Even if you are now more than willing to make sacrifices for your friends, what is demanded of you could be just too great. Rather than doing too much for them, be prepared to accept their offers of help. Care is required in financial deals at the moment, particularly if you are not absolutely sure of yourself.

31 WEDNESDAY ☿ *Moon Age Day 20   Moon Sign Cancer*

Getting what you want from life could suddenly be much easier, especially if you are not very demanding at present and are happier with a simple way of going on. Money is, if anything, not really an issue under present trends. What appeals to you the most in life at the moment is likely to cost you nothing.

November
2007

1 THURSDAY ☿ *Moon Age Day 21   Moon Sign Cancer*

Trends encourage you to start the new month with plenty of zest but also with a little caution. If you decide to go with the flow for once, you may fail to look at issues with the same sort of discrimination you usually would. Even friends can be evasive, and though they mean you no harm, you need to check what they are saying.

2 FRIDAY ☿ *Moon Age Day 22   Moon Sign Leo*

There's no doubt about it, Sagittarius can be extremely curious right now. If you want to know what makes everything tick, you probably won't be happy to settle for compromises. In matters of love you can show a cheerful and co-operative face and may be undertaking little tasks that you know will please your partner.

3 SATURDAY *Moon Age Day 23   Moon Sign Leo*

Why not do what you can to ring the changes, and in particular take advantage of any opportunity to travel? There are gains to be made as a result of your forethought and forward planning, and you should be looking and feeling good in all social situations. A day to keep up your efforts to please your sweetheart.

4 SUNDAY *Moon Age Day 24   Moon Sign Virgo*

Even if your ideas are big, you do have what it takes to see them through to completion. This might be slightly more awkward on a Sunday because you are less likely to be at work. All the same, there are things you can do, as well as taking full advantage of any offer that seems to be potentially exciting.

5 MONDAY
Moon Age Day 25   Moon Sign Virgo

It is possible you have already used up the sparklers across the weekend, and probably just as well because the planetary line-up for today is not exactly right for a rip-roaring firework party! You could use this fairly quiet interlude to spend some time either in isolation or else merely with one special person.

6 TUESDAY
Moon Age Day 26   Moon Sign Libra

As an antidote to yesterday you can now make sure that something approaching the full force of the Sagittarian nature is now evident once again. You may not take kindly to being told what to do right now, and if anyone is going to offering advice and generally ruling the roost, it is almost certain to be the Archer.

7 WEDNESDAY
Moon Age Day 27   Moon Sign Libra

Trends suggest that what interests you the most today is being involved in mental pursuits of some sort. The more you are stimulated the better you should feel, and you may not be too pleased if everything is sorted out immediately. You need a challenge, and if one isn't forthcoming of its own accord you have scope to find one nevertheless.

8 THURSDAY
Moon Age Day 28   Moon Sign Libra

There is a slight tendency for you to be rather outspoken today and you may get on the wrong side of someone else as a result. The Archer is often inclined to act on impulse, but present trends show how much better life would be if you learned to think ahead and to act with circumspection.

9 FRIDAY
Moon Age Day 0   Moon Sign Scorpio

A day to look out for familiar faces and to make the most of the help that you can obtain from people who clearly do have your best interests at heart. You may not be working at your very best and may be somewhat quieter as a result of the position of the Moon in your solar chart.

10 SATURDAY
Moon Age Day 1   Moon Sign Scorpio

Probably the greatest motivation for today is a burning desire to help others, but you can do so in a quiet and unobtrusive way. The weekend could offer some exciting diversions, though you might be more likely to take up what is on offer tomorrow. For the moment you can simply afford to plod along happily.

11 SUNDAY
Moon Age Day 2   Moon Sign Sagittarius

All of a sudden life seems to be filled with potential and is likely to be far more stimulating than seems to have been the case across the last few days. Where there isn't any real incentive to do something exciting, you have the ability to find reasons yourself and to be very responsive to the needs of others right now.

12 MONDAY
Moon Age Day 3   Moon Sign Sagittarius

Your strength lies in keeping faith with your own thoughts and being willing to push your luck a little. Dealing with a wealth of different jobs at the same time should be easy for you, and you can make the day a whirl of activity. You respond well to any sort of challenge around now and will love to be put in a position that means thinking on your feet.

13 TUESDAY
Moon Age Day 4   Moon Sign Sagittarius

You should start as you mean to go on today, and shouldn't have any problem at all confronting issues that may have seemed somewhat uncomfortable only a few days ago. This early part of the working week offers the best incentives for getting ahead at work, even if social trends are confused and rather fraught.

14 WEDNESDAY
Moon Age Day 5   Moon Sign Capricorn

Your judgement is potentially sound, which is why you should know instinctively that your decisions are good and that others should follow your lead. That's fine, but you will need to put your point of view across in a fairly diplomatic way, particularly if there are some very sensitive types to be dealt with.

15 THURSDAY   *Moon Age Day 6   Moon Sign Capricorn*

If personal finances seem to be slightly less secure right now, you may decide to draw in your horns a little. It isn't very long until Christmas and you should look carefully at that list of potential presents before you start spoiling yourself in any way. Personality clashes are possible later in the day.

16 FRIDAY   *Moon Age Day 7   Moon Sign Aquarius*

You might be so busy today that you won't have enough time to notice what friends and colleagues need. That would be a pity because you are probably in the perfect position to lend a hand. Your mind may already be on the weekend and some exciting possibility that lies in store.

17 SATURDAY   *Moon Age Day 8   Moon Sign Aquarius*

Your persuasive powers are well starred, so if there is anything you really want, this is the time to go out and ask for it. Very few people could withstand a frontal approach by you under present trends, and you can use the simple fact of your popularity to help you to get what you are looking for.

18 SUNDAY   *Moon Age Day 9   Moon Sign Aquarius*

The real Sagittarius can be put on display at the moment. You should be warm and kind, but at the same time capable of inspiring a great deal of excitement wherever you go. If this happens to be a working day for you there is no doubt about your ability to get on. The sort of Sunday you get is directly responsive to your own attitude.

19 MONDAY   *Moon Age Day 10   Moon Sign Pisces*

Your main objectives and ideas are the ones that count, so now is the time to set to with a will and don't take no for an answer unless you know that there is no point in chasing something any further. It is definitely wise to realise when you are beaten and to simply move on in another more fruitful direction.

20 TUESDAY   *Moon Age Day 11   Moon Sign Pisces*

Now you can make the most of a much deeper sense of belonging, and might decide to spend more time thinking about family matters and resolving any difficulties from the recent past. Even if you remain generally active in a work sense, don't be surprised if a large part of your mind is elsewhere.

21 WEDNESDAY   *Moon Age Day 12   Moon Sign Aries*

Trends encourage a desire for freedom, though you may not have enough clear space in your life to push forward in any tangible way. Rather than getting bogged down with pointless details, why not be willing to look at the broad prospects for the present and future? Someone you see very rarely could be paying a return visit to your life.

22 THURSDAY   *Moon Age Day 13   Moon Sign Aries*

It is unlikely that you would have much difficulty standing up for yourself today, but there is a slight danger that you may be defending yourself before you are actually attacked. Try to remain calm under all circumstances and look at the deeper issues involved in your life.

23 FRIDAY   *Moon Age Day 14   Moon Sign Taurus*

If there is one thing you have scope to strive for at the moment it is efficiency. This can be slightly frustrating if everyone else you encounter seems to be very confused and inclined to make constant mistakes. The wearing fact is having to do your own job but at the same time to keep an eye on colleagues.

24 SATURDAY   *Moon Age Day 15   Moon Sign Taurus*

The weekend could bring a sigh of relief if you know you are going to have a few hours during which to please yourself. If you feel you are in need of a total break, it's worth allowing others to take some of the domestic strain whilst you put your feet up. Of course for the Archer this could also mean finding excitement.

25 SUNDAY   *Moon Age Day 16   Moon Sign Gemini*

As the Moon moves into your opposite zodiac sign, you have a chance to slow down and take stock of situations. A day to spend some time with your family and allow life to flow over you if this proves to be possible. Be prepared to look ahead and plan for the future, with a particular eye on Christmas, which is only a month away.

26 MONDAY   *Moon Age Day 17   Moon Sign Gemini*

Even if this isn't a very dynamic start to a new week, as the day wears on you can ensure you are more aware of what needs doing and how you should go about dealing with situations. At least you needn't let the lunar low break down your basic optimism this time round.

27 TUESDAY   *Moon Age Day 18   Moon Sign Cancer*

Life can seem fairly disheartening in a practical sense, but that shouldn't really matter, particularly if you are filled with new ideas and chasing these throughout most of the day. If there are small failures, you can afford to dismiss these from your mind quickly and move on to newer and more exciting possibilities.

28 WEDNESDAY   *Moon Age Day 19   Moon Sign Cancer*

Trying to remain open-minded might be difficult for colleagues and family members, which is why you could have to work that much harder on their account. Your attitude is good and you have what it takes to talk someone out of a depression – even if you have to work extra hard to achieve your objective.

29 THURSDAY   *Moon Age Day 20   Moon Sign Leo*

If there is anything that proves to be problematic today it is likely to be emotional relationships. Even if you personally remain optimistic and happy, the same may not be true of everyone who is dear to you. Once again it's possible that much of your time is spent supporting others.

30 FRIDAY
Moon Age Day 21   Moon Sign Leo

There is much potential for romantic developments today and a great desire to push the bounds of the credible in a practical way. Newer and better possibilities seem to stand around every corner, and for the first time in quite a few days you can make sure that others are also seeing a brighter sky.

December

2007

1 SATURDAY
Moon Age Day 22   Moon Sign Virgo

With a great sense of urgency you have scope to plough into family life and home-based practical necessities this weekend. You are well aware that December has now arrived and might be putting some thought into Christmas. Trends indicate an accident-prone tendency, so it's worth taking extra care.

2 SUNDAY
Moon Age Day 23   Moon Sign Virgo

Communication is once again the main feature of life and you might be quite happy to chew the fat all day if circumstances allow. Lady Archers in particular might decide to indulge in a shopping spree, and all Sagittarians have an opportunity to preen themselves, possibly in advance of some sort of social occasion.

3 MONDAY
Moon Age Day 24   Moon Sign Virgo

You could turn this into a period of significant domestic rewards and make the most of the positive trends that stand around at the moment. Outside of the house you would be wise to play things closer to your chest than might normally be the case and probably create a deliberate air of mystery!

4 TUESDAY
Moon Age Day 25   Moon Sign Libra

Getting more out of life is about giving over a greater percentage of the day to recreation of some sort. You will only become bored if you commit yourself to work all the time, and would be much better off splitting your time as best you can. Even if not everyone is on your side at the moment, you can make sure the important people will be.

149

5 WEDNESDAY   *Moon Age Day 26   Moon Sign Libra*

There are some surprises possible as far as your social life is concerned, and in terms of activities you may have already begun the run-up to Christmas. Committing yourself exclusively to your work might be as difficult today as it has been so far this week, and your best approach is to try for some variety.

6 THURSDAY   *Moon Age Day 27   Moon Sign Scorpio*

Trends offer a quieter interlude, which you can use to spend some time sitting alone and thinking. There is no problem about this because even the Archer needs periods of reflection, and these are much more likely at times when the Moon is occupying your solar twelfth house.

7 FRIDAY   *Moon Age Day 28   Moon Sign Scorpio*

There may be additions coming along in the family, or else family members taking up with new relationships. Somewhere along the line you are going to have to open your heart to someone you didn't know before. Thank heavens you are a Sagittarian, because such matters should be child's play to you.

8 SATURDAY   *Moon Age Day 29   Moon Sign Scorpio*

Slowly but surely you are able to turn your mind outward and should gradually become less inclined to spend moments on your own. Nevertheless you can still be quite contemplative and enjoy a very happy state, halfway between your own little world and the outside one that demands your attention.

9 SUNDAY   *Moon Age Day 0   Moon Sign Sagittarius*

The Moon returns to your zodiac sign, bringing the lunar high for December. Everything will seem a riot of colour, and there isn't much doubt about your general commitment to life across the board. Now is the time for maximum effort at work and for proving how capable you really are.

10 MONDAY   *Moon Age Day 1   Moon Sign Sagittarius*

What matters most about your nature at the moment is how original you prove to be. This enables you to attract others and achieve a popularity that is stunning, even by your standards. If you can imagine something today, there is a very real possibility that you can actually do it. Obstructions seem to evaporate.

11 TUESDAY   *Moon Age Day 2   Moon Sign Capricorn*

Now is the time during December when you need to be very careful about what you are spending. The necessities of Christmas, together with a natural tendency to spread money around, are a powerful and difficult combination. Before committing yourself to any purchase, it's worth asking yourself if it is really necessary.

12 WEDNESDAY   *Moon Age Day 3   Moon Sign Capricorn*

When it comes to romance you could well be entering the most positive phase for some time. You can make best use of this by noticing what is going on around you and registering the compliments you can attract from a number of different directions. You have everything it takes to turn heads.

13 THURSDAY   *Moon Age Day 4   Moon Sign Capricorn*

Coming to a final decision regarding a personal matter might prove to be slightly difficult, and you will have to think carefully before committing yourself to any course of action today. Don't be too quick to make a judgement about the actions of a friend or colleague, and where possible give them the benefit of the doubt.

14 FRIDAY   *Moon Age Day 5   Moon Sign Aquarius*

Be prepared to get your ideas across in a big way. Even if you are enjoying the run-up to Christmas in some ways, in others all the socialising does tend to get in the way. As usual you are willing to commit yourself to new plans and altered strategies, but others may be much less inclined to do so.

15 SATURDAY   *Moon Age Day 6   Moon Sign Aquarius*

It looks as though you are on a drive to get as many of the good things of life as you can. This is fine, but there are times today when you may realise that material considerations are far less important than sometimes seems to be the case. You might decide to spend a good deal of your time today helping others.

16 SUNDAY   *Moon Age Day 7   Moon Sign Pisces*

What a good time this would be for simply talking. You have scope to chat to loved ones and to friends, and to put your point of view in a rational and a humorous way. Confidence tends to be fairly high at the moment, and you shouldn't be suffering too much from doubts or anxieties.

17 MONDAY   *Moon Age Day 8   Moon Sign Pisces*

Make the most of an assertive start to the week as far as you are concerned. There are positive trends around at the moment which encourage a stronger than usual desire to get ahead. The only slight problem comes if circumstances seem to conspire against you. If this happens, frustration is a distinct possibility.

18 TUESDAY   *Moon Age Day 9   Moon Sign Aries*

There are signs that pleasant social activities surround you, which is fine as long as you have the time to take part in them. There could be moments today when you wish everyone would stop enjoying themselves and get down to some real work. Even if you aren't exactly isolating yourself, you can afford to keep up the pressure.

19 WEDNESDAY   *Moon Age Day 10   Moon Sign Aries*

With one-to-one relationships now more important than ever, your strength lies in finding new ways to express your love and in offering compliments. Maybe you are slightly insecure in one way or another, and it's worth being slightly more circumspect than is sometimes the case.

20 THURSDAY   *Moon Age Day 11   Moon Sign Taurus*

If you want to achieve important things early next year, now is the time to start putting in the necessary effort. No matter how much you are committed to the festive season, in one way or another you need to look beyond it. Avoid getting tied up in red tape at any stage around now.

21 FRIDAY   *Moon Age Day 12   Moon Sign Taurus*

Even if you remain generally optimistic, this might be more than can be said for the people with whom you mix on a daily basis. Actually, the fact that some of them seem slightly down in the dumps could have something to do with your own actions. Your best response is to talk things through and see what you can do to help.

22 SATURDAY   *Moon Age Day 13   Moon Sign Gemini*

You would be wise not to expect too much today because the lunar low is around. At least you will get it out of the way before Christmas arrives and you could probably do with a couple of quieter days in any case. You can gain support when you need it the most, and might decide to simply sit and watch on occasion today.

23 SUNDAY   *Moon Age Day 14   Moon Sign Gemini*

It's not worth trying to push yourself too hard for the moment. You need to be fairly circumspect, and could get a great deal from being in the bosom of the family. The big day is nearly at hand, so why not wrap up those last presents and get yourself prepared for what can be a hectic but enjoyable time to come?

24 MONDAY   *Moon Age Day 15   Moon Sign Cancer*

It looks as though you can now get yourself back on form and be more than willing to enjoy whatever life throws at you. The quiet Archer has now disappeared and you can afford to be making more noise than just about anyone else. By all means give yourself a pat on the back for anything you achieve today in record time.

25 TUESDAY   *Moon Age Day 16   Moon Sign Cancer*

It's Christmas Day and the planets align themselves to offer you a satisfying and happy sort of time. If not everyone is responding in quite the way you might have wished, you have the ability to take such matters well in your stride. Don't overstuff yourself with food, and try to get at least some exercise later in the day.

26 WEDNESDAY   *Moon Age Day 17   Moon Sign Leo*

Trends herald a restless interlude, and you may decide to make at least a short journey to see someone who lives at a distance. Sticking around home all the time will probably bore you, so if you have no choice, find something useful and interesting to do. Entertaining younger family members might be a start.

27 THURSDAY   *Moon Age Day 18   Moon Sign Leo*

Even if you are somewhat happier with your domestic lot than seems to have been the case yesterday, you still have the need for new stimulus in your life and can easily become bored with routines. Physical activity is an ideal option, and this should form part of your response.

28 FRIDAY   *Moon Age Day 19   Moon Sign Leo*

There are signs that your mind is often elsewhere today, and that those around you who want to attract your attention might have some small problems in doing so. Personalities abound but for the moment you may be slightly stuck inside your own head. Maybe you could use this period to think about things you want to do in the future.

29 SATURDAY   *Moon Age Day 20   Moon Sign Virgo*

The festive season goes on, and you might even spend much of your time today thinking up new ways to make people happy. A lighter touch is possible on your part, and you should be less inclined to look inside yourself too much. Personal attachments really count, and you have what it takes to show your love in practically everything you do.

30 SUNDAY   *Moon Age Day 21   Moon Sign Virgo*

Today responds best if you are busy, and you might be dreaming up all manner of possibilities in order to distract yourself. The Christmas holidays are great in theory but they often turn out to be too long for your impetuous nature. Once you are settled on something you find interesting and stimulating, you have scope to be more contented.

31 MONDAY   *Moon Age Day 22   Moon Sign Libra*

The last day of the year offers you an opportunity to dream up ever more exciting possibilities for the new year. You can contribute well to any festivities that take place this evening, but bear in mind that the planets favour a slightly more abstemious approach this time around!